BY BRENÉ BROWN

DARE TO LEAD

BRAVING THE WILDERNESS

RISING STRONG

DARING GREATLY

THE GIFTS OF IMPERFECTION

I THOUGHT IT WAS JUST ME

THE GIFTS OF
IMPERFECTION

Brené Brown

PhD, LMSW

10th Anniversary Edition

THE GIFTS OF
IMPERFECTION

RANDOM HOUSE • NEW YORK

Published in the United States by
Random House, an imprint and division of
Penguin Random House LLC, New York.

RANDOM HOUSE and the HOUSE colophon are
registered trademarks of Penguin Random House LLC.

Originally published in the United States
by Hazelden Publishing in 2010.

LIBRARY OF CONGRESS CATALOGING-IN-PUBLICATION DATA
Brown, Brené
The gifts of imperfection: let go of who you think
you're supposed to be and embrace who you are / by Brené Brown.
p.   cm.
Includes bibliographical references.
ISBN 978-0-593-13358-3 (hardcover)
ISBN 978-0-593-13359-0 (ebook)
1. Self-acceptance. 2. Self-esteem. I. Title.
BF575.S37B76 2010
158—dc22   2010016989

Printed in the United States of America on acid-free paper

randomhousebooks.com

98

2020 Random House Hardcover Edition

To Steve, Ellen, and Charlie.
I love you with my whole heart.

CONTENTS

10TH ANNIVERSARY NOTE
FROM BRENÉ

It's been thirteen years since my 2007 ~~Breakdown~~ Spiritual Awakening and a full decade since I wrote *The Gifts*.

~~Life has been good. I mean it's been so easy and just about perfect since I started cultivating all of the great practices on the wholehearted list and letting go of all of the fear-based behaviors from the "shit list" that I write about in this book. It's like once you work your way through these ten guideposts, everything just falls in place. No more shame. No more anxiety. No more self-loathing. No more crushing busyness. No more "never enough."~~

Sigh.

In the past thirteen years, I have loved, lost, fallen down too many times to count, mercifully gotten back up that same incalculable number of times, broken my toes, broken my own heart, and had a couple of other people break it for me. I dropped my daughter off at college then stayed in bed crying for a week, fell back in love with Steve, questioned how Steve and I are ever going to stay married and how we should split the albums during the divorce, wrote four more books, lost track of a million great ideas and found ten good ones, buried people I love including parents, watched Charlie turn into an amazing teenager, lost my first pet, bought reading glasses, white-knuckled my sobriety, discovered that sobriety is my superpower, planned interventions, wondered if I needed an intervention, fought for social justice, continued to uncover more blind spots and areas of unacknowledged privilege, moved houses, started businesses, shut down businesses, swam in several pools of low-grade depression, splashed around in my magic Lake Travis with the people I love the most, practiced gratitude for every single gift in my life, and pissed and moaned for so long about the smallest irritations that I actually got sick of hearing myself complain.

It's been a full, amazing, hard-as-shit, beautiful thirteen years. Most days, I'd describe it as a wonderful life with really painful patches. However, not gonna lie—there are seasons when it feels like the painful patches will swallow us whole and I'm not sure how to scratch my way back to a balanced life, much less a "wonderful life." In fact, as I'm writing this, I'm quarantined with my family in the midst of the COVID-19 pandemic, and I'm getting ready for a podcast interview with Dr. Ibram X. Kendi on antiracism. It's June 3, 2020, and I want to believe so badly we're going to get through this pandemic and things will *not* return to normal. That we will become a country ready to own our history and do what it takes to put an end to the policies and practices that not only dehumanize the Black community but all of the communities that have suffered under white supremacy.

When I look back on the past decade and think about the work, research, and words that make up the original *Gifts of Imperfection* book, there are two things that are gratifyingly and painfully clear to me:

1. Transforming the ten guideposts of wholehearted living into daily, lifelong practices is more work than I ever imagined.

2. Transforming the ten guideposts of wholehearted living into daily, lifelong practices is more valuable than I ever imagined.

It's not hyperbole to say that writing *The Gifts* changed my life and continues to do so. The adventure of wholehearted living launched my work, continues to inform my relationship with Steve, helps me find the courage to be the parent I want to be and the grace to try again when I'm not, and, most of all, this work continues to lead me back to myself. All of myself—the parts I love and the parts I've orphaned and keep bringing back home so I can wipe their noses, bandage their skinned knees, and be whole.

I wrote *The Gifts* in my early forties. Ellen was eleven years old when it came out, and Charlie was only five. Now Ellen is a senior in college, and Charlie is about to start high school. I haven't changed the stories or much of the text. The lessons are the same even though the kids are older, Steve and I have more wrinkles and gray hair, and some of the concepts have become the foundation of entire books.

INTEGRATION

When we talked to readers about the 10th Anniversary Edition, people were very clear that the text shouldn't change. This book has become a reference guide and touchstone for many people, and we want to honor this. We did, however, add a new Integration Index so that you, as a reader, can start to embed the work in your life.

When we were doing the research for *Rising Strong,* we discovered more about how creativity is the engine that drives integration; it helps us transform knowledge into practice. Basically, we move what we're learning from our heads to our hearts through our hands.

The index in the back of the book is adapted from a system that I heard Maria Popova explain to Tim Ferriss during a podcast in 2014. Maria is a writer, poet, cultural critic, and the genius curator behind brainpickings.org, a newsletter and online publication that has been added to the Library of Congress's permanent digital archive of culturally valuable materials.

This was six years ago, and Maria may no longer use this approach; however, for those of us who spent many hours wondering how she tracked, connected, and wove together all of the source materials she shares on brainpickings.org, it was a brilliant illumination.

In the podcast, Maria explained that when you read a book, you walk away with certain takeaways that are thematically linked. In most books, these takeaways don't occur sequentially. An alternative index is based on ideas that are important to you—not just keywords—so a personalized

index allows you to find and document the patterns that create personal meaning and understanding. I started creating
alternative indexes, and it's transformed the way I read,
learn, research, and integrate work. For example, in Ibram
Kendi's book *How to Be an Antiracist,* my index included the
following:

> Beautiful language (borrowed this one from Maria):
> Don't understand—need to learn more:
> FD (stands for family dinner—something I want to
>   discuss as a family):
> Had no idea:
> More books to read:
> Organizational culture change:
> Quotes:
> RHR (this stands for rabbit hole research—it's my
>   way of saying I want to look at original source
>   material):
> Share with Steve:
> SO HARD:

Next to these, I have a list of page numbers separated by
commas (e.g., 13, 46, 167, 229). When I turn to those pages
(which I mark with tiny Post-it tabs), I see the highlighted
passages. I'm telling you—it's a miracle. When you're done,
you have new information *and* a blueprint of how to integrate
it into your life.

For this book, I'm giving you pages and a list of suggested
index ideas based on how I've seen thousands of people integrate this work into daily practices. I think there's some po-

etry in the fact that the Latin root of the word *integrate* is *integrare,* which means "to make whole." *How do we use what we're learning about wholeheartedness to actually make ourselves more whole?*

There are two other integration tools that will help you own and embody this work. First, we've spent several years building, testing, and validating our Wholehearted Inventory, which consists of ten subscales that align with the guideposts. This free online instrument will allow you to assess your strengths and opportunities for growth around the main topics explored in the book. I recommend you make this inventory before you start reading. It's useful to engage with it after you've finished, but I think it's more useful to go into the book knowing where you've already got skills and where you can build them.

You can find that at brenebrown.com/wholeheartedinventory.

Another integration tool that we're building for you is a free online workshop that will launch in the fall of 2020. We'll walk through the ten guideposts, I'll take questions (and ask questions), and we'll DIG deep together.

WITH OUR WHOLE HEARTS

Over the past ten years, I've had the great honor of teaching and facilitating my work on courage and vulnerability all over the world. Although I am a teacher and a researcher, these experiences always afford me the opportunity to learn far more than I teach. One thing that's become very clear to me is that the experience of sharing our vulnerability is not the same for all of us. Let me explain.

The greatest casualty of trauma—the thing that trauma often takes away from us—is the emotional, and sometimes even physical, safety that is necessary for us to be vulnerable. I've seen this in my work with the military, veterans, and survivors. And, in addition to the trauma of violence, neglect and poverty are trauma. Dehumanization—the core of racism, sexism, homophobia, transphobia, xenophobia, and all systemic forms of oppression and/or bias—is a form of daily trauma. You only have to witness someone who shares your identity suffering to experience real emotional and physical trauma.

Many of these systemic forms of trauma are so pervasive that asking people to embrace vulnerability and imperfections without taking into consideration their lived experience can be asking them to do something that is not emotionally or even physically safe in all environments.

So, what do we do? I believe that everyone deserves brave and safe spaces to be vulnerable. None of us can fully embrace the gifts of vulnerability, courage, and authenticity if any of us are denied those gifts because of who we are or what we've endured. Being imperfect, authentic, and vulnerable is a function of being human—not a privilege afforded to those who can get away with it without being labeled, dismissed, and judged.

We are all responsible for creating these brave, safe spaces and dismantling the systems that perpetuate trauma. Living and loving with our whole hearts is not just about self-work. It's how we change the world. Without awareness, work, and actionable change, we will continue to live in a world where we perceive some people as brave and strong for sharing their vulnerabilities, while for others, their sharing of struggles and fears becomes confirmation of the conscious or unconscious biases we hold.

The experiences that bring the most meaning to our lives are born of vulnerability—and that includes freedom. And, as Rev. Dr. Martin Luther King, Jr. famously said, "No one is free until we are all free." There is no wholeheartedness unless we do everything we can to dismantle the brokenheartedness of injustice.

I still use the definition of authenticity that I first wrote for this book as a personal prayer. So, holding these words in my heart and in my hand, here's my prayer for all of us and my daily commitment:

May we find the courage to let go of who we think we're supposed to be so that we can fully embrace our authentic selves—the imperfect, the creative, the vulnerable, the powerful, the broken, and the beautiful.

May we show ourselves and others the compassion that comes from knowing that we are all made of strength and struggle.

May we create a just and equitable world where privilege isn't a prerequisite for self-expression and authenticity, where everyone feels invited and safe to express their power and their vulnerability.

And last, may we experience the strength of connection, the love of belonging, and the grace of pure joy.

Thank you for walking with me.

PREFACE

Owning our story and loving ourselves
through that process is the bravest thing
that we will ever do.

Once you see a pattern, you can't *un*-see it. Trust me, I've tried. But when the same truth keeps repeating itself, it's hard to pretend that it's just a coincidence. For example, no matter how hard I try to convince myself that I can function on six hours of sleep, anything less than eight hours leaves me impatient, anxious, and foraging for carbohydrates. It's a pattern. I also have a terrible procrastination pattern: I always put off writing by reorganizing my entire house and spending way too much time and money buying office supplies and organizing systems. Every single time.

One reason it's impossible to un-see trends is that our minds are engineered to seek out patterns and to assign meaning to them. Humans are a meaning-making species. And, for better or worse, my mind is actually fine-tuned to do this. I spent years training for it, and now it's how I make my living.

As a researcher, I observe human behavior so I can identify and name the subtle connections, relationships, and patterns that help us make meaning of our thoughts, behaviors,
and feelings.

I love what I do. Pattern hunting is wonderful work and, in
fact, throughout my career, my attempts at un-seeing were
strictly reserved for my personal life and those humbling vulnerabilities that I loved to deny. That all changed in November 2006, when the research that fills these pages smacked
me upside the head. For the first time in my career, I was
desperate to un-see my own research.

Up until that point, I had dedicated my career to studying
difficult emotions like shame, fear, and vulnerability. I had
written academic pieces on shame, developed a shame-
resilience curriculum for mental health and addictions professionals, and written a book about shame resilience called *I
Thought It Was Just Me.*[1]

In the process of collecting thousands of stories from a di-
verse group of research participants who lived all over the
country—ranging in age from eighteen to eighty-seven—I saw
new patterns that I wanted to know more about. Yes, we all
struggle with shame and the fear of not being enough. And,
yes, many of us are afraid to let our true selves be seen and
known. But in this huge mound of data there was also story
after story of people who were living these amazing and inspiring lives.

I heard stories about the power of embracing imperfection
and vulnerability. I learned about the inextricable connection
between joy and gratitude, and how things that I take for
granted, like rest and play, are as vital to our health as nutri-

tion and exercise. These research participants trusted themselves, and they talked about authenticity and love and belonging in a way that was completely new to me.

I wanted to look at these stories as a whole, so I grabbed a file and a Sharpie and wrote the first word that came to my mind on the tab: *wholehearted*. I wasn't sure what it meant yet, but I knew that these stories were about people living and loving with their whole hearts.

I had a lot of questions about wholeheartedness. What did these folks value? How did they create all of this resilience in their lives? What were their main concerns and how did they resolve or address them? Can anyone create a wholehearted life? What does it take to cultivate what we need? What gets in the way?

As I started analyzing the stories and looking for reoccurring themes, I realized that the patterns generally fell into one of two columns; for simplicity's sake, I first labeled these *Do* and *Don't*. The *Do* column was brimming with words like worthiness, rest, play, trust, faith, intuition, hope, authenticity, love, belonging, joy, gratitude, and creativity. The *Don't* column was dripping with words like perfection, numbing, certainty, exhaustion, self-sufficiency, being cool, fitting in, judgment, and scarcity.

I gasped the first time I stepped back from the poster paper and took it all in. It was the worst kind of sticker shock. I remember mumbling, "No. No. No. How can this be?"

Even though I wrote the lists, I was shocked to read them. When I code data, I go into deep researcher mode. My only focus is on accurately capturing what I heard in the stories. I don't think about how I would say something, only how the research participants said it. I don't think about what an experience would mean to me, only what it meant to the person who told me about it.

I sat in the red chair at my breakfast room table and stared at these two lists for a very long time. My eyes wandered up and down and across. I remember at one point I was actually sitting there with tears in my eyes and with my hand across my mouth, like someone had just delivered bad news.

And, in fact, it was bad news. I thought I'd find that wholehearted people were just like me and doing all of the same things I was doing: working hard, following the rules, doing it until I got it right, always trying to know myself better, raising my kids exactly by the books . . .

After studying tough topics like shame for a decade, I truly believed that I deserved confirmation that I was "living right."

But here's the tough lesson that I learned that day (and every day since):

> How much we know and understand ourselves is critically important, but there is something that is even more essential to living a wholehearted life: loving ourselves.

Knowledge is important, but only if we're being kind and gentle with ourselves as we work to discover who we are. Wholeheartedness is as much about embracing our tenderness and vulnerability as it is about developing knowledge and claiming power.

And perhaps the most painful lesson of that day hit me so hard that it took my breath away: It was clear from the data that we cannot give our children what we don't have. Where we are on our journey of living and loving with our whole hearts is a much stronger indicator of parenting success than anything we can learn from how-to books.

This journey is equal parts heart work and head work, and as I sat there on that dreary November day, it was clear to me that I was lacking in my own heart work.

I finally stood up, grabbed my marker off the table, drew a line under the *Don't* list, and then wrote the word *me* under the line. My struggles seemed to be perfectly characterized by the sum total of the list.

I folded my arms tightly across my chest, sunk deep down into my chair, and thought, *This is just great. I'm living straight down the shit list.*

I walked around the house for about twenty minutes trying to un-see and undo everything that had just unfolded, but I couldn't make the words go away. I couldn't go back, so I did the next best thing: I folded all of the poster sheets into neat squares and tucked them into a Rubbermaid tub that fit nicely under my bed, next to my Christmas wrap. As I shoved the tub under the bed, I would never have guessed that it would be over a year before I looked at these data again.

Next, I got myself a really good therapist and began a year of serious soul work that would forever change my life. Diana, my therapist, and I still laugh about my first visit. Diana, who is a therapist to many therapists, started with the requisite, "So what's going on?" I pulled out a smaller version of the *Do* list and matter-of-factly said, "I need more of the things on this list. Some specific tips and tools would be helpful. Nothing deep. No childhood crap or anything."

It was a long year. I lovingly refer to it as the 2007 ~~Break-down~~ Spiritual Awakening. It felt like a textbook breakdown to me, but Diana called it a spiritual awakening. I think we were both right. In fact, I'm starting to question if you can have one without the other.

Of course, it's not a coincidence that this unraveling happened in November 2006. The stars were perfectly aligned for a breakdown: I was raw from being newly sugar and flour free, I was days away from my birthday (always a contemplative time for me), I was burned out from work, and I was right on the cusp of my *midlife unraveling*.

People may call what happens at midlife "a crisis," but it's not. It's an unraveling—a time when you feel a desperate pull to live the life you want to live, not the one you're "supposed" to live. The unraveling is a time when you are challenged by the universe to let go of who you think you are supposed to be and to embrace who you are.

Midlife is certainly one of the great unraveling journeys, but there are others that happen to us over the course of our lives:

- marriage
- divorce
- becoming a parent
- recovery
- moving
- an empty nest
- retiring
- experiencing loss or trauma
- working in a soul-sucking job

The universe is not short on wake-up calls. We're just quick to hit the snooze button.

As it turned out, the work I had to do was messy and deep. I slogged through it until one day, exhausted and with mud still wet and dripping off of my traveling shoes, I realized, "Oh, my God. I feel different. I feel joyful and real. I'm still afraid, but I also feel really brave. Something has changed— I can feel it in my bones."

I was healthier, more joyful, and more grateful than I had ever felt. I felt calmer and grounded, and significantly less anxious. I had rekindled my creative life, reconnected with my family and friends in a new way, and most important, felt truly comfortable in my own skin for the first time in my life.

I learned how to worry more about how I felt and less about "what people might think." I was setting new boundaries and began to let go of my need to please, perform, and perfect. I started saying *no* rather than *sure* (and being resentful and pissed off later). I began to say "Oh, hell yes!" rather than "Sounds fun, but I have lots of work to do" or "I'll do that when I'm _____ (thinner, less busy, better prepared)."

As I worked through my own wholehearted journey with Diana, I read close to forty books, including every spiritual awakening memoir I could get my hands on. They were incredibly helpful guides, but I still craved a guidebook that could offer inspiration and resources, and basically serve as a soul traveler's companion of sorts.

One day, as I stared at the tall pile of books precariously stacked on my nightstand, it hit me! *I want to tell this story in a memoir.* I'll tell the story of how a cynical, smart-ass academic became every bit of the stereotype that she spent her entire adult life ridiculing. I'll fess up about how I became the middle-aged, recovering, health-conscious, creative, touchy-feely spirituality-seeker who spends days contemplating things like grace, love, gratitude, creativity, authenticity, and is happier than I imagined possible. I'll call it *Wholehearted*.

I also remember thinking, *Before I write the memoir, I need to use this research to write a guidebook on whole-hearted living!* By mid-2008, I had filled three huge tubs with notebooks, journals, and mounds of data. I had also done countless hours of new research. I had everything I needed, including a passionate desire to write the book that you're holding in your hands.

On that fateful November day when the list appeared and I sunk into the realization that I wasn't living and loving with my whole heart, I wasn't totally convinced. Seeing the list wasn't enough to fully believe in it. I had to dig very deep and make the *conscious choice* to believe . . . to believe in myself and the possibility of living a different life. A lot of questioning, countless tears, and a huge collection of joyful moments later, believing has helped me see.

I now see how owning our story and loving ourselves through that process is the bravest thing that we will ever do.

I now see that cultivating a wholehearted life is not like trying to reach a destination. It's like walking toward a star in the sky. We never really arrive, but we certainly know that we're heading in the right direction.

I now see how gifts like courage, compassion, and connection only work when they are exercised. Every day.

I now see how the work of *cultivating* and *letting go* that shows up in the ten guideposts is not "to-do list" material. It's not something we accomplish or acquire and then check off our list. It's life work. It's soul work.

For me, believing was seeing. I believed first, and only then I was able to see how we can truly change ourselves, our families, and our communities. We just have to find the courage to live and love with our whole hearts. It's an honor to make this journey with you!

THE GIFTS OF
IMPERFECTION

Wholehearted Living

Wholehearted living is about engaging in our lives from a place of worthiness. It means cultivating the courage, compassion, and connection to wake up in the morning and think, *No matter what gets done and how much is left undone, I am enough.* It's going to bed at night thinking, *Yes, I am imperfect and vulnerable and sometimes afraid, but that doesn't change the truth that I am also brave and worthy of love and belonging.*

THE JOURNEY

Wholehearted living is not a onetime choice. It is a process. In fact, I believe it's the journey of a lifetime. My goal is to bring awareness and clarity to the constellation of choices that lead to wholeheartedness and to share what I've learned from many, many people who have dedicated themselves to living and loving with their whole hearts.

Before embarking on any journey, including this one, it's important to talk about what we need to bring along. What does it take to live and love from a place of worthiness? How do we embrace imperfection? How do we cultivate what we need and let go of the things that are holding us back? The answers to all of these questions are courage, compassion, and connection—the tools we need to work our way through our journey.

If you're thinking, *Great. I just need to be a superhero to fight perfectionism,* I understand. Courage, compassion, and connection seem like big, lofty ideals. But in reality, they are daily practices that, when exercised enough, become these incredible gifts in our lives. And the good news is that our vulnerabilities are what force us to call upon these amazing tools. Because we're human and so beautifully imperfect, we get to practice using our tools on a daily basis. In this way, courage, compassion, and connection become gifts—the gifts of imperfection.

Here's what you'll find in the pages that follow. In the first chapter, I explain what I've learned about courage, compassion, and connection and how they are truly the tools for developing worthiness.

Once we get some clarity about the tools that we're going to use on this journey, in the next chapter we move to the heart of the matter: love, belonging, and worthiness. I answer some of the most difficult questions of my career: What is love? Can we love someone and betray them? Why does our constant need to fit in sabotage real belonging? Can we love the people in our lives, like our partners and children, more than we love ourselves? How do we define worthiness, and why do we so often end up hustling for it rather than believing in it?

We encounter obstacles on every journey we make; the wholehearted journey is no exception. In the next chapter, we'll explore what I've found to be the greatest barriers to living and loving with our whole hearts and how we can develop effective strategies to move through the barriers and to cultivate resilience.

From there, we'll explore the ten guideposts for the wholehearted journey, daily practices that provide direction for our journey. There's one chapter for each guidepost, and each chapter is illustrated with stories, definitions, quotes, and ideas for making deliberate and inspired choices about the way we live and love.

DEFINING MOMENTS

This book is full of big-concept words such as *love, belonging,* and *authenticity.* I think it's critically important to define the gauzy words that are tossed around every day but rarely explained. And I think good definitions should be accessible and actionable. I've tried to define these words in a way that will help us unpack the term and explore the pieces. When we dig down past the feel-good words and excavate the daily activities and experiences that put the *heart* in wholehearted living, we can see how people define the concepts that drive their actions, beliefs, and emotions.

For example, when the research participants talked about a concept such as *love,* I was careful to define it as they experienced it. Sometimes that required developing new definitions (like I actually did with *love* and many other words). Other times, when I started looking around in the existing literature, I found definitions that captured the spirit of the participants' experiences. A good example of this is *play*. Play is an essential component of wholehearted living, and when I researched the topic, I discovered the amazing work of Dr. Stuart Brown.[1] So, rather than creating a new definition, I reference his work because it accurately reflects what I learned in the research.

I realize that definitions spark controversy and disagreement, but I'm okay with that. I'd rather we debate the meaning of words that are important to us than not discuss them at all. We need common language to help us create awareness and understanding, which is essential to wholehearted living.

DIGGING DEEP

In early 2008, when my blog was still pretty new, I wrote a post about breaking my "dig-deep" button. You know the dig-deep button, right? It's the button that you rely on when you're too bone-tired to get up one more time in the middle of the night or to do one more load of throw-up-diarrhea laundry or to catch one more plane or to return one more call or to please/perform/perfect the way you normally do even when you just want to flip someone off and hide under the covers.

The dig-deep button is a secret level of pushing through when we're exhausted and overwhelmed, and when there's too much to do and too little time for self-care.

In my blog post, I explained how I had decided not to fix my dig-deep button. I made a promise to myself that when I felt emotionally, physically, and spiritually done, I'd try slowing down rather than relying on my old standbys: pushing through, soldiering on, and sucking it up.

It worked for a while, but I missed my button. I missed having something to turn to when I was depleted and down. I needed a tool to help me dig my way out. So, I turned back to my research to see if I could find a way to dig that was more consistent with wholehearted living. Maybe there was something better than just sucking it up.

Here's what I found: People who live wholeheartedly do indeed DIG Deep. They just do it in a different way. When they're exhausted and overwhelmed, they get

DELIBERATE in their thoughts and behaviors
through prayer, meditation, or simply setting their
intentions;
INSPIRED to make new and different choices;
GOING. They take action.

Since I made that discovery, I've been DIGging Deep the new way, and it's been pretty amazing. One example happened just recently when I was lost in an Internet fog. Rather than working, I was just lulling myself into a haze by mindlessly playing on Facebook and piddling on the computer. It was neither relaxing nor productive—it was just a giant time and energy suck.

I tried the new DIG Deep—get deliberate, inspired, and going. I told myself, "If you need to refuel and losing yourself online is fun and relaxing, then do it. If not, do something deliberately relaxing. Find something inspiring to do rather than something soul-sucking. Then, last but not least, get up and do it!" I closed my laptop, said a little prayer to remind myself to be self-compassionate, and watched a movie on Netflix that I'd been dying to see. It was exactly what I needed.

It wasn't the old Dig Deep—the pushing through. I didn't force myself to start working or to do something productive. Rather, I prayerfully, intentionally, and thoughtfully did something restorative.

Each guidepost has a DIG Deep section to help us start thinking about how we get deliberate and inspired about our choices, and how we take action. I share my personal DIG Deep strategies with you and I encourage you to come up with your own. These new strategies have been so much more effective than the old "pushing through."

WHAT I HOPE TO CONTRIBUTE

This book is full of powerful topics such as self-compassion, acceptance, and gratitude. I'm not the first to talk about these subjects, and I'm certainly not the smartest researcher or the most talented writer. I am, however, the first to explain how these topics work individually and together to cultivate wholehearted living. And, maybe more important, I'm certainly the first person to come at these topics from the perspective of someone who has spent years studying shame and fear.

I can't tell you how many times I wanted to give up my research on shame. It's extremely difficult to dedicate your career to studying topics that make people squeamish. On several occasions I've literally thrown my hands up and said, "I quit. It's too hard. There are so many cool things to study. I want out of this!" I didn't choose to study shame and fear; the research chose me.

Now I know why. It was what I needed—professionally and personally—to prepare for this work on wholehearted-ness. We can talk about courage and love and compassion until we sound like a greeting card store, but unless we're willing to have an honest conversation about what gets in the way of putting these into practice in our daily lives, we will never change. Never, ever.

Courage sounds great, but we need to talk about how it requires vulnerability and the willingness to let go of what other people think, and for most of us, that's scary. Compassion is something we all want, but are we willing to look at why boundary-setting and saying *no* is a critical component of compassion? Are we willing to say *no,* even if we're disappointing someone? Belonging is an essential component of wholehearted living, but first we have to cultivate self-acceptance—why is this such a struggle?

Before I start writing, I always ask myself, "Why is this book worth writing? What's the contribution that I'm hoping to make?" Ironically, I think the most valuable contribution that I can make to the ongoing discussions about love, belonging, and worthiness stems from my experiences as a shame researcher.

Coming at this work with a full understanding of how the shame tapes and gremlins keep us feeling afraid and small allows me to do more than present great ideas; this perspective helps me share real strategies for changing our lives. If we want to know why we're all so afraid to let our true selves be seen and known, we have to understand the power of shame and fear. If we can't stand up to the *never good enough* and *who do you think you are?* we can't move forward.

I only wish that during those desperate and defeated moments of my past, when I was knee-deep in shame research, I could have known what I know now. If I could go back and whisper in my ear, I'd tell myself the same thing that I'll tell you as we begin this journey:

> Owning our story can be hard but not nearly as difficult as spending our lives running from it. Embracing our vulnerabilities is risky but not nearly as dangerous as giving up on love and belonging and joy—the experiences that make us the most vulnerable. Only when we are brave enough to explore the darkness will we discover the infinite power of our light.

Courage, Compassion, and Connection:
The Gifts of Imperfection

Practicing courage, compassion, and connection in our daily lives is how we cultivate worthiness. The key word is *practice*. Mary Daly, a theologian, writes, "Courage is like— it's a habitus, a habit, a virtue: You get it by courageous acts. It's like you learn to swim by swimming. You learn courage by couraging." The same is true for compassion and connection. We invite compassion into our lives when we act compassionately toward ourselves and others, and we feel connected in our lives when we reach out and connect.

Before I define these concepts and talk about how they work, I want to show you how they work together in real life—as practices. This is a personal story about the courage to reach out, the compassion that comes from saying, "I've been there," and the connections that fuel our worthiness.

THE GUN-FOR-HIRE SHAME STORM

Several years ago, the principal of a large public elementary school and the president of the school's parent-teacher organization (PTO) invited me to speak to a group of parents about the relationship between resilience and boundaries. I was in the process of collecting data about wholehearted parenting and schools at the time, so I was excited about the opportunity. I had no idea what I was getting myself into.

The second I walked into the school auditorium, I felt this really strange vibe from the parents in the audience. They almost seemed agitated. I asked the principal about it, and she just shrugged her shoulders and walked away. The PTO president didn't have much to say about it either. I chalked it up to my nerves and tried to let it go.

I was sitting in the front row when the principal introduced me. This is always a very awkward experience for me. Someone is running through a list of my accomplishments while I'm secretly trying to stave off vomiting and talking myself out of running. Well, this introduction was beyond anything I had ever experienced.

The principal was saying things like, "You might not like what you're going to hear tonight, but we need to listen for the sake of our children. Dr. Brown is here to transform our school and our lives! She's going to set us straight whether we like it or not!"

She was talking in this loud, aggressive voice that made her seem downright pissed off. I felt like I was being introduced for WWE WrestleMania. All we needed were a few strobe lights.

In hindsight, I should have walked up to the podium and said, "I'm feeling very uncomfortable. I'm excited to be here, but I'm certainly not here to set anyone straight. I also don't want you to think that I'm trying to transform your school in an hour. What's going on?"

But I didn't. I just started talking in my vulnerable I'm-a-researcher-but-I'm-also-a-struggling-parent way. Well, the die had been cast. These parents were not receptive. Instead, I felt row after row of people glaring at me.

One man, who was sitting right up front, had his arms folded across his chest and his teeth clenched so tightly that the veins in his neck were popping out. Every three or four minutes he'd shift in his seat, roll his eyes, and sigh louder than I've ever heard anyone sigh. It was so loud that I'm barely comfortable calling it a sigh. It was more like a *humph!* It was so bad that the people next to him were visibly mortified by his behavior. They were still inexplicably unhappy with me, but he was making the entire evening unbearable for all of us.

As an experienced teacher and group leader, I know how to handle these situations and am normally comfortable doing so. When someone is being disruptive, you really only have two choices: ignore them or take a break so that you can privately confront them about their inappropriate behavior. I was so knocked off my game by this weird experience that I did the very worst thing possible: I tried to impress him.

I started talking louder and getting really animated. I quoted scary research statistics that would freak out any parent. I served up my authenticity for a big ole helping of *You better listen to me or your kids are going to drop out of third grade and take up hitchhiking, drugs, and running with scissors.*

Nothing. Nada.

I didn't get a head nod or a slight grin or anything. I just managed to freak out the other 250 already-pissy parents. It was a disaster. Trying to co-opt or win over someone like that guy is always a mistake, because it means trading in your authenticity for approval. You stop believing in your worthiness and start hustling for it. And, oh man, was I hustling.

The second the talk ended, I grabbed my stuff and ran-walked to my car. As I was pulling out of the parking lot, my face was growing hotter. I felt small and my heart was racing. I tried to push back the instant replay of me acting crazy, but I couldn't stop thinking about it. The shame storm was brewing.

When the shame winds are whipping all around me, it's almost impossible to hold on to any perspective or to recall anything good about myself. I went right into the bad self-talk of *God, I'm such an idiot. Why did I do that?*

The greatest gift of having done this work (the research and the personal work) is that I can recognize shame when it's happening. First, I know my physical symptoms of shame—the dry mouth, time slowing down, tunnel vision, hot face, racing heart. I know that playing the painful slow-motion reel over and over in my head is a warning sign.

I also know that the very best thing to do when this is happening feels totally counterintuitive: Practice courage and reach out! We have to own our story and share it with someone who has earned the right to hear it, someone whom we can count on to respond with compassion. We need courage, compassion, and connection. ASAP.

Shame hates it when we reach out and tell our story. It hates having words wrapped around it—it can't survive being shared. Shame loves secrecy. The most dangerous thing to do after a shaming experience is hide or bury our story. When we bury our story, the shame metastasizes. I remember saying out loud: "I need to talk to someone RIGHT NOW. Be brave, Brené!"

But here's the tricky part about compassion and connecting: We can't call just anyone. It's not that simple. I have a lot of good friends, but there are only a handful of people whom I can count on to practice compassion when I'm in the dark shame place.

If we share our shame story with the wrong person, they can easily become one more piece of flying debris in an already dangerous storm. We want solid connection in a situation like this—something akin to a sturdy tree firmly planted in the ground. We definitely want to avoid the following:

1. ***I feel sorry for you*** · sympathy versus empathy

    The person who responds with sympathy ("I feel so sorry for you") rather than empathy ("I get it, I feel with you, and I've been there"). The subtext of this response is distance: These things don't happen to me or to people like me. If you want to see a shame cyclone turn deadly, throw one of these at it: "Oh, you poor thing" or "Bless your heart."

2. ***You "should" feel shame!*** · judgment

    The person who hears the story and actually feels shame for you. The friend gasps and confirms how horrified you should be. Then there is an awkward silence. Then you have to make this person feel better by convincing them that you're not a terrible person.

3. *You've let me down* • disappointment

    The person who needs you to be the pillar of worthiness and authenticity. This person can't help you because they are too disappointed in your imperfections. You've let this person down.

4. *This feels terrible. Who can we blame? You?* • discharging discomfort with blame

    Because shame is visceral and contagious, we can feel it for other people. This person immediately needs to discharge the discomfort and vulnerability of the situation by blaming and scolding. They may blame/scold you: "What were you thinking?" Or they may look for someone else to take the fall: "Who was that guy? We'll kick his butt." Caution: Parents can fall easily into this when a child shares a shaming story with them. "How did you let this happen?"

5. *Let's make this go away* • minimizing/avoiding

    We minimize and avoid when we want hard feelings to go away. Out of their own discomfort, this person refuses to acknowledge that you're in pain and/or that you're hurting: "You're exaggerating. It wasn't that bad. You rock. You're perfect. Everyone loves you."

6. *If you think that's bad!* • comparing/competing

This person confuses "connecting with you over shared experiences" with the opportunity to one-up you. "That's nothing. Listen to what happened to me one time!"

7. *Don't upset people or make them uncomfortable* • speaking truth to power

You hold someone accountable for language, comments, or behavior that marginalizes or dehumanizes others, and it causes discomfort or conflict. When this person observes this or hears your story of what happened, they respond with, "I can't believe you said that to your boss!" or "I can't believe you went there!" or "You can't talk about that stuff with people," versus an empathic response of "That must have been hard—you were really brave" or "It's hard to stand up for what you believe in— thank you."

8. *I can fix this and I can fix you* • advice-giving/ problem-solving

Sometimes when we see pain our first instinct is to fix it. This is especially true for those of us whom people seek out to help with problem-solving. In these instances, rather than listen and be with people in their emotions, we start fixing.

Of course, we're all capable of being "these friends"—especially if someone tells us a story that gets right up in our own shame grille. We're human, imperfect, and vulnerable. It's hard to practice compassion when we're struggling with our authenticity or when our own worthiness is off balance.

When we're looking for compassion, we need someone who is deeply rooted, able to bend, and, most of all, we need someone who embraces us for our strengths and struggles. We need to honor our struggle by sharing it with someone who has *earned* the right to hear it. When we're looking for compassion, it's about connecting with the *right person* at the *right time* about the *right issue*.

I called my sister. It's only been since the 2007 ~~Breakdown~~ Spiritual Awakening that I've called one of my sisters or my brother for shame-cyclone support. I'm four years older than my brother and eight years older than my sisters (they're twins). Before 2007, I was pretty vested in being the older, perfect (aka uptight, better than, and judgmental) sister.

Ashley was amazing. She listened and responded with total compassion. She had the courage to tap into her own struggles with worthiness so that she could genuinely connect to what I was experiencing. She said wonderfully honest and empathic things like, "Oh, man. That's so hard. I've done that dance. I hate that feeling!" That may not be what someone else would need to hear, but for me it was the best.

Ashley wasn't uprooted and thrown into the storm created

by my experience. She also wasn't so rigid that she snapped with judgment and blame. She didn't try to fix me or make me feel better; she just listened and had the courage to share some of her own vulnerabilities with me.

I felt totally exposed and completely loved and accepted at the same time (which is the definition of compassion for me). Trust me when I tell you that shame and fear can't tolerate that kind of powerful connection surging between people. That's exactly why courage, compassion, and connection are the tools we need for the wholehearted journey. To top it off, my willingness to let someone I care about see me as imperfect led to a strengthening of our relationship that continues today—that's why I can call courage, compassion, and connection the gifts of imperfection. When we're willing to be imperfect and real, these gifts just keep giving.

Just a quick follow-up to the story: About a week after the wrestling match/parenting talk, I found out that the school was experiencing a hovering problem—parents were in the classrooms all day and interfering with instruction and class management. Without telling me, the principal and PTO president had required the parents to attend my lecture. They told the parents that I was coming to tell them why they needed to stop hovering. In other words, I was set up as a helicopter-parent mercenary. Not good. I may not be a fan of hovering in the classroom, but I'm also not a parenting gun-for-hire. The irony is that I had no idea that was an issue, so I never even mentioned the topic.

With this story in mind, let's take a closer look at each of the concepts of wholeheartedness and how they work together.

COURAGE

Courage is a huge theme in my life. It seems that either I'm praying for some, feeling grateful for having found a little bit, appreciating it in other people, or studying it. I don't think that makes me unique. Everyone wants to be brave.

After interviewing people about the truths of their lives— their strengths and struggles—I realized that courage is one of the most important qualities that wholehearted people have in common. And not just any kind of courage; I found that wholeheartedness requires *ordinary courage*. Here's what I mean . . .

The root of the word *courage* is *cor*—the Latin word for *heart*. In one of its earliest forms, the word *courage* had a very different definition than it does today. Courage originally meant "To speak one's mind by telling all one's heart." Over time, this definition has changed, and, today, courage is more synonymous with being heroic. Heroics is important and we certainly need heroes, but I think we've lost touch with the idea that speaking honestly and openly about who we are, about what we're feeling, and about our experiences (good and bad) is the definition of courage. Heroics is often about putting our life on the line. Ordinary courage is about putting our *vulnerability* on the line. In today's world, that's pretty extraordinary.[1]

When we pay attention, we see courage every day. We see it when people reach out for help, like I did with Ashley. I see it in my classroom when a student raises their hand and says, "I'm completely lost. I have no idea what you're talking about." Do you know how incredibly brave it is to say "I don't know" when you're pretty sure everyone around you gets it? Of course, from my decades of teaching, I know that if one person can find the courage to say, "You've lost me," there are probably at least ten more students who feel the exact same way. They may not take the risk, but they certainly benefit from that one person's courage.

I saw courage in my daughter, Ellen, when she called me from a slumber party at 10:30 p.m. and said, "Mom, can you come get me?" When I picked her up, she got in the car and said, "I'm sorry. I just wasn't brave enough. I got homesick. It was so hard. Everyone was asleep, and I had to walk to Libby's mom's bedroom and wake her up."

I pulled into our driveway, got out of the car, and walked around to the backseat where Ellen was sitting. I scooted her over and sat next to her. I said, "Ellen, I think asking for what you need is one of the bravest things that you'll ever do. I suffered through a couple of really miserable sleepovers and slumber parties because I was too afraid to ask to go home. I'm proud of you."

The next morning during breakfast, Ellen said, "I thought about what you said. Can I be brave again and ask for something else?" I smiled. "I have another slumber party next weekend. Would you be willing to pick me up at bedtime? I'm just not ready." That's courage. The kind we could all use more of.

I also see courage in myself when I'm willing to risk being vulnerable and disappointed. For many years, if I really wanted something to happen—an invitation to speak at a special conference, a promotion, a radio interview—I pretended that it didn't matter that much. If a friend or colleague would ask, "Are you excited about that television interview?" I'd shrug it off and say, "I'm not sure. It's not that big of a deal." Of course, in reality, I was praying that it would happen.

It's only been in the last few years that I've learned that playing down the exciting stuff doesn't take the pain away when it doesn't happen. It does, however, minimize the joy when it does happen. It also creates a lot of isolation. Once you've diminished the importance of something, your friends are not likely to call and say, "I'm sorry that didn't work out. I know you were excited about it."

Now when someone asks me about a potential opportunity that I'm excited about, I'm more likely to practice courage and say, "I'm so excited about the possibility. I'm trying to stay realistic, but I really hope it happens." When things haven't panned out, it's been comforting to be able to call a supportive friend and say, "Remember that event I told you about? It's not going to happen, and I'm so disappointed."

I also witnessed another example of ordinary courage at my son Charlie's preschool. Parents were invited to attend a holiday music presentation put on by the kids. You know the scene—twenty-five children singing with fifty-plus parents, grandparents, and siblings in the audience wielding thirty-nine phones. The parents were holding up cameras in the air and randomly snapping pictures while they scrambled to make sure that their kids knew they were there and on time.

In addition to all the commotion in the audience, one three-year-old girl, who was new to the class, cried her way through the entire performance because she couldn't see her mom from the makeshift stage. As it turns out, her mother was stuck in traffic and missed the performance. By the time

COURAGE, COMPASSION, AND CONNECTION   23

her mother arrived, I was kneeling by the classroom door telling Charlie good-bye. From my low vantage point, I watched the girl's mother burst through the door and immediately start scanning the room to find her daughter. Just as I was getting ready to stand up and point her toward the back of the classroom where a teacher was holding her daughter, another mother walked by us, looked straight at this stressed mom, shook her head, and rolled her eyes.

I stood up, took a deep breath, and tried to reason with the part of me that wanted to chase after the better-than-you eye-rolling mom and kick her perfectly punctual ass. Just then two more moms walked up to this now tearful mother and smiled. One of the mothers put her hand on top of the woman's shoulder and said, "We've all been there. I missed the last one. I wasn't just late. I completely forgot." I watched as the woman's face softened, and she wiped away a tear. The second woman looked at her and said, "My son was the only one who wasn't wearing pajamas on PJ Day—he still tells me it was the most rotten day ever. It will be okay. We're all in the same boat."

By the time this mother made it to the back of the room where the teacher was still comforting her daughter, she looked calm. Something that I'm sure came in handy when her daughter lunged for her from about six feet away. The moms who stopped and shared their stories of imperfection and vulnerability were practicing courage. They took the time to stop and say, "Here's my story. You're not alone." They didn't have to stop and share; they could have easily joined the perfect-parent parade and marched right by her.

As these stories illustrate, courage has a ripple effect.

Every time we choose courage, we make everyone around us a little better and the world a little braver. And our world could stand to be a little kinder and braver.

COMPASSION

To prepare for writing my book on shame, I read everything I could find on compassion. I ultimately found a powerful fit between the stories I heard in the interviews and the work of American Buddhist nun Pema Chödrön. In her book *The Places That Scare You,* Chödrön writes, "When we practice generating compassion, we can expect to experience the fear of our pain. Compassion practice is daring. It involves learning to relax and allow ourselves to move gently toward what scares us."[2]

What I love about Chödrön's definition is her honesty about the vulnerability of practicing compassion. If we take a closer look at the origin of the word *compassion,* much like we did with *courage,* we see why compassion is not typically our first response to suffering. The word *compassion* is derived from the Latin words *pati* and *cum,* meaning "to suffer with." I don't believe that compassion is our default response. I think our first response to pain—ours or someone else's—is to self-protect. We protect ourselves by looking for someone or something to blame. Or sometimes we shield ourselves by turning to judgment or by immediately going into fix-it mode.

Chödrön addresses our tendency to self-protect by teaching that we must be honest and forgiving about when and how we shut down: "In cultivating compassion we draw from the wholeness of our experience—our suffering, our empathy, as well as our cruelty and terror. It has to be this way. Compassion is not a relationship between the healer and the wounded. It's a relationship between equals. Only when we know our own darkness well can we be present with the darkness of others. Compassion becomes real when we recognize our shared humanity."[3]

In my story, Ashley was willing to be in my darkness with me. She wasn't there as my helper or to fix me; she was just with me—as an equal—holding my hand as I waded through my feelings.

BOUNDARIES AND COMPASSION

One of the greatest (and least discussed) barriers to compassion practice is the fear of setting boundaries and holding people accountable. I know it sounds strange, but I believe that understanding the connection between boundaries, accountability, acceptance, and compassion has made me a kinder person. Before the breakdown, I was sweeter—judgmental, resentful, and angry on the inside, but sweeter on the outside. Today, I think I'm genuinely more compassionate, less judgmental and resentful, and way more serious about boundaries. I have no idea what this combination looks like on the outside, but it feels pretty powerful on the inside.

Before this research, I knew a lot about each one of these concepts, but I didn't understand how they fit together. During the interviews, it blew my mind when I realized that many of the truly committed compassion practitioners were also the most boundary-conscious people in the study. Compassionate people are boundaried people. I was stunned.

Here's what I learned: The heart of compassion is really

acceptance. The better we are at accepting ourselves and others, the more compassionate we become. Well, it's difficult to accept people when they are hurting us or taking advantage of us or walking all over us. This research has taught me that if we really want to practice compassion, we have to start by setting boundaries and holding people accountable for their behavior.

We live in a blame culture—we want to know whose fault it is and how they're going to pay. In our personal, social, and political worlds, we do a lot of screaming and finger-pointing, but we rarely hold people accountable. How could we? We're so exhausted from ranting and raving that we don't have the energy to develop meaningful consequences and enforce them. From Washington, DC, and Wall Street to our own schools and homes across the globe, I think this rage-blame-too-tired-and-busy-to-follow-through mind-set is why we're so heavy on self-righteous anger and so low on compassion.

Wouldn't it be better if we could be kinder, but firmer? How would our lives be different if there were less blame and more accountability? What would our work and home lives look like if we judged less but had more respect for boundaries?

I was recently brought in to talk with a group of corporate leaders who were trying to manage a difficult reorganization in their company. One of the project managers told me that, after listening to me talk about the dangers of using shame as a management tool, he was worried that he shamed his team members. He told me that when he gets really frustrated, he singles people out and criticizes their work in team meetings.

He explained, "I'm so frustrated. I have two employees who just don't listen. I explain every single detail of the project, I check to make sure they understand, and they *still* do it their way. I'm out of options. I feel backed into a corner and angry, so I take them down in front of their colleagues."

When I asked him how he was holding these two employees accountable for not following the project protocol, he replied, "What do you mean by accountable?"

I explained, "After you check with them to make sure they understand your expectations and the objectives, how do you explain the consequences of not following the plan or not meeting the objectives?"

He said, "I don't talk about the consequences. They know they're supposed to follow the protocol."

I gave him an example. "Okay. What would happen if you told them that you were going to write them up or give them an official warning the next time they violated protocol and that if it continues, they're going to lose their jobs?"

He shook his head and said, "Oh, no. That's pretty serious. I'd have to get the human resources people involved. That becomes a big hassle."

Setting boundaries and holding people accountable is a lot more work than shaming and blaming. But it's also much more effective. Shaming and blaming without accountability is toxic to couples, families, organizations, and communities. First, when we shame and blame, it moves the focus from the original behavior in question to our own behavior. By the time this boss is finished shaming and humiliating his employees in front of their colleagues, the only behavior in question is his.

Additionally, if we don't follow through with appropriate consequences, people learn to dismiss our requests—even if they sound like threats or ultimatums. If we ask our kids to keep their clothes off the floor and they know that the only consequence of not doing it is a few minutes of yelling, it's fair for them to believe that it's really not that important to us.

It's hard for us to understand that we can be compassionate and accepting while we hold people accountable for their behaviors. We can, and, in fact, it's the best way to do it. We can confront someone about their behavior, or fire someone, or fail a student, or discipline a child without berating them or putting them down. The key is to separate people from their behaviors—to address what they're doing, not who they are (I'll talk more about this in the next chapter). It's also important that we can lean into the discomfort that comes with straddling compassion and boundaries. We have to stay away from convincing ourselves that we hate someone or that they deserve to feel bad so that we can feel better about holding them accountable. That's where we get into trouble. When we talk ourselves into disliking someone so we're more comfortable holding them accountable, we're priming ourselves for the shame and blame game.

When we fail to set boundaries and hold people accountable, we feel used and mistreated. This is why we sometimes attack who they are, which is far more hurtful than addressing a behavior or a choice. For our own sake, we need to understand that it's dangerous to our relationships and our well-being to get mired in shame and blame, or to be full of self-righteous anger. It's also impossible to practice compassion from a place of resentment. If we're going to practice acceptance and compassion, we need boundaries and accountability.

CONNECTION

I define *connection* as *the energy that exists between people when they feel seen, heard, and valued; when they can give and receive without judgment; and when they derive sustenance and strength from the relationship.*

Ashley and I felt deeply connected after our experience. I know I was seen, heard, and valued. Even though it was scary, I was able to reach out for support and help. And we both felt strengthened and fulfilled. In fact, a couple of weeks later, Ashley said, "I can't tell you how glad I am that you called me that day. It helped me so much to know that I'm not the only one who does stuff like that. I also love knowing that I can help you and that you trust me." Connection begets connection.

As a matter of fact, we are wired for connection. It's in our biology. From the time we are born, we need connection to thrive emotionally, physically, spiritually, and intellectually. A decade ago, the idea that we're "wired for connection" might have been perceived as touchy-feely or a good branding slogan. Today, we know that the need for connection is more than a feeling or a hunch. It's hard science. Neuroscience, to be exact.

In his book *Social Intelligence: The New Science of Human Relationships,* Daniel Goleman explores how the latest findings in biology and neuroscience confirm that we are hardwired for connection and that our relationships shape our biology as well as our experiences. Goleman writes, "Even our most routine encounters act as regulators in the brain, priming our emotions, some desirable, others not. The more strongly connected we are with someone emotionally, the greater the mutual force."[4] It's amazing—yet perhaps not surprising—that the connectedness we experience in our relationships impacts the way our brain develops and performs.

Our innate need for connection makes the consequences of disconnection that much more real and dangerous. Sometimes we only *think* we're connected. Technology, for instance, has become a kind of imposter for connection, making us believe we're connected when we're really not—at least not in the ways we need to be. In our technology-crazed world, we've confused being communicative with feeling connected. Just because we're plugged in doesn't mean we feel seen and heard. In fact, hyper-communication can mean we spend more time on Facebook than we do face-to-face with the people we care about. I can't tell you how many times I've walked into a restaurant and seen two parents on their cell phones while their kids are busy texting or playing video games. What's the point of even sitting together?

As we think about the definition of connection and how easy it is to mistake technology for connecting, we also need to consider letting go of the myth of self-sufficiency. One of the greatest barriers to connection is the cultural importance we place on "going it alone." Somehow we've come to equate success with not needing anyone. Many of us are willing to extend a helping hand, but we're very reluctant to reach out for help when we need it ourselves. It's as if we've divided the world into "those who offer help" and "those who need help." The truth is that we are both.

I've learned so much about giving and receiving from the research participants who are engaged in wholehearted living but nothing more important than this:

Until we can receive with an open heart, we are never really giving with an open heart. When we attach judgment to receiving help, we knowingly or unknowingly attach judgment to giving help.

For years, I placed value on being the helper in my family. I could help with a crisis or lend money or dispense advice. I was always happy to help others, but I would have never called my siblings to ask them for help, especially for support during a shame storm. At the time, I would have vehemently denied attaching judgment to my generous giving. But now, I understand how I derived self-worth from never needing help and always offering it.

During the breakdown, I needed help. I needed support and handholding and advice. Thank God! Turning to my younger brother and sisters completely shifted our family dynamics. I gained permission to fall apart and be imperfect, and they could share their strength and incredible wisdom with me. If connection is the energy that surges between people, we have to remember that those surges must travel in both directions.

The wholehearted journey is not the path of least resistance. It's a path of consciousness and choice. And, to be honest, it's a little counterculture. The willingness to tell our stories, feel the pain of others, and stay genuinely connected in this disconnected world is not something we can do halfheartedly.

To practice courage, compassion, and connection is to look at life and the people around us, and say, "I'm all in."

Exploring the Power of Love, Belonging, and Being Enough

Love is the most important thing in our lives, a passion for which we would fight or die, and yet we're reluctant to linger over its names. Without a supple vocabulary, we can't even talk or think about it directly.

—DIANE ACKERMAN

Love and belonging are essential to the human experience. As I conducted my interviews, I realized that only *one thing* separated the research participants who felt a deep sense of love and belonging from the people who seem to be struggling for it. That one thing is the belief in their worthiness. It's as simple and complicated as this: If we want to fully experience love and belonging, we must believe that we are *worthy* of love and belonging.

When we can let go of what other people think and own our story, we gain access to our worthiness—the feeling that we are enough just as we are and that we are worthy of love and belonging. When we spend a lifetime trying to distance ourselves from the parts of our lives that don't fit with who we think we're supposed to be, we stand outside of our story and hustle for our worthiness by constantly performing, perfecting, pleasing, and proving. Our sense of worthiness—that critically important piece that gives us access to love and belonging—lives inside of our story.

The greatest challenge for most of us is believing that we are worthy *now,* right this minute. Worthiness doesn't have prerequisites. So many of us have knowingly created/unknowingly allowed/been handed down a long list of worthiness prerequisites:

- I'll be worthy when I lose twenty pounds.
- I'll be worthy if I can get pregnant.
- I'll be worthy if I get/stay sober.
- I'll be worthy if everyone thinks I'm a
  good parent.
- I'll be worthy when I can make a living
  selling my art.
- I'll be worthy if I can hold my marriage together.
- I'll be worthy when I make partner.
- I'll be worthy when my parents finally approve.
- I'll be worthy if he calls back and asks me out.
- I'll be worthy when I can do it all and look like
  I'm not even trying.

Here's what is truly at the *heart* of wholeheartedness: Worthy now. Not if. Not when. We are worthy of love and belonging *now.* Right this minute. As is.

In addition to letting go of the ifs and whens, another critical piece of owning our story and claiming our worthiness is cultivating a better understanding of love and belonging. Oddly enough, we desperately need both but rarely talk about what they really are and how they work. Let's take a look.

DEFINING LOVE AND BELONGING

For years I avoided using the word *love* in my research because I didn't know how to define it, and I wasn't sure that "C'mon, you know, *love*" as a definition would fly. I also couldn't rely on quotes or song lyrics, however much they might inspire me and speak truth to me. It's not my training as a researcher.

As much as we need and want love, we don't spend much time talking about what it means. Think about it. You might say "I love you" every day, but when's the last time you had a serious conversation with someone about the meaning of love? In this way, love is the mirror image of shame. We desperately don't want to experience shame, and we're not willing to talk about it. Yet the only way to resolve shame is to talk about it. Maybe we're afraid of topics like love and shame. Most of us like safety, certainty, and clarity. Shame and love are grounded in vulnerability and tenderness.

Belonging is another topic that is essential to the human experience but rarely discussed.

Most of us use the terms *fitting in* and *belonging* interchangeably, and like many of you, I'm really good at fitting in. We know exactly how to hustle for approval and acceptance.

We know what to wear, what to talk about, how to make people happy, what not to mention—we know how to chameleon
our way through the day.

One of the biggest surprises in this research was learning
that fitting in and belonging are not the same thing, and, in
fact, fitting in gets in the way of belonging. Fitting in is about
assessing a situation and becoming who you need to be to be
accepted. Belonging, on the other hand, doesn't require us to
change who we are; it requires us to *be* who we are.

Before I share my definitions with you, I want to point out
three issues that I'm willing to call truths.

Love and belonging will always be uncertain. Even
though connection and relationship are the most critical
components of life, we simply *cannot* accurately measure
them. Relational concepts don't translate into bubbled answer sheets. Relationship and connection happen in an inde-
finable space between people, a space that will never be fully
known or understood by us. Everyone who risks explaining
love and belonging is hopefully doing the best they can to answer an unanswerable question. Myself included.

Love belongs with belonging. One of the most surprising things that unfolded in my research is the pairing of certain terms. I can't separate the concepts of love and belonging
because when people spoke of one, they always talked about
the other. The same holds true for the concepts of joy and
gratitude, which I'll talk about in a later chapter. When emotions or experiences are so tightly woven together in people's
stories that they don't speak of one without the other, it's not
an accidental entanglement; it's an intentional knot. Love belongs with belonging.

Of this, I am actually certain. After collecting thousands of stories, I'm willing to call this a fact: **A deep sense of love and belonging is an irreducible human need from the moment we're born until the day we die.** We are biologically, cognitively, physically, and spiritually wired to love, to be loved, and to belong. When those needs are not met, we don't function as we were meant to. We break. We fall apart. We numb. We ache. We hurt others. We get sick. There are certainly other causes of illness, numbing, and hurt, but the absence of love and belonging will always lead to suffering.

It took me three years to whittle these definitions and concepts from a decade of interviews. Let's take a look.

Love:

We cultivate love when we allow our most vulnerable and powerful selves to be deeply seen and known, and when we honor the spiritual connection that grows from that offering with trust, respect, kindness, and affection.

Love is not something we give or get; it is something that we nurture and grow, a connection that can only be cultivated between two people when it exists within each one of them—we can only love others as much as we love ourselves.

Shame, blame, disrespect, betrayal, and the withholding of affection damage the roots from which love grows. Love can only survive these injuries if they are acknowledged, healed, and rare.

Belonging:

Belonging is the innate human desire to be part of something larger than us. Because this yearning is so primal, we often try to acquire it by fitting in and by seeking approval, which are not only hollow substitutes for belonging, but often barriers to it. Because true belonging only happens when we present our authentic, imperfect selves to the world, our sense of belonging can never be greater than our level of self-acceptance.

One reason that it takes me so long to develop these concepts is that I often don't want them to be true. It would be different if I studied the effect of bird poop on potting soil, but this stuff is personal and often painful. Sometimes, as I turned to the data to craft definitions like the ones above, I would cry. I didn't want my level of self-love to limit how much I can love my children or my husband. Why? Because loving them and accepting their imperfections is much easier than turning that light of loving-kindness on myself.

If you look at the definition of love and think about what it means in terms of self-love, it's very specific. Practicing self-love means learning how to trust ourselves, to treat ourselves with respect, and to be kind and affectionate toward ourselves. This is a tall order given how hard most of us are on ourselves. I know I can talk to myself in ways that I would never consider talking to another person. How many of us are quick to think, *God, I'm so stupid* and *Man, I'm such an idiot*?

Just like calling someone we love stupid or an idiot would be incongruent with practicing love, talking like that to ourselves takes a serious toll on our self-love.

It's worth noting that I use the words *innate* and *primal* in the definition of belonging. I'm convinced that belonging is in our DNA, most likely connected to our most primitive survival instinct. Given how difficult it is to cultivate self-acceptance in our perfectionist society and how our need for belonging is hardwired, it's no wonder that we spend our lives trying to fit in and gain approval.

It's so much easier to say, "I'll be whoever or whatever you need me to be, as long as I feel like I'm part of this." From group-think to gossiping, we'll do what it takes to fit in if we believe it will meet our need for belonging. But it doesn't. We can only belong when we offer our most authentic selves and when we're embraced for who we are.

PRACTICING LOVE AND BELONGING

To begin by always thinking of love as an action rather than a feeling is one way in which anyone using the word in this manner automatically assumes accountability and responsibility.

—BELL HOOKS[1]

While I have personally and professionally agonized over the definitions of love and belonging, I have to admit that they have fundamentally changed the way I live and parent. When I'm tired or stressed, I can be mean and blaming—especially toward my husband, Steve. If I truly love Steve (and, oh man, I do), then how I behave every day is as important, if not more important, than saying "I love you" every day. When we don't practice love with the people we claim to love, it takes a lot out of us. Incongruent living is exhausting.

It's also pushed me to think about the important differences between *professing* love and *practicing* love. During a recent radio interview about the rash of celebrity infidelities, the host asked me, "Can you love someone and cheat on them or treat them poorly?"

I thought about it for a long time, then gave the best answer I could based on my work: "I don't know if you can love someone and betray them or be cruel to them, but I do know that when you betray someone or behave in an unkind way toward them, you are not practicing love. And, for me, I don't just want someone who says they love me; I want someone who practices that love for me every day."

In addition to helping me understand what love looks like between people, these definitions also forced me to acknowledge that cultivating self-love and self-acceptance is not optional. They aren't endeavors that I can look into if and when I have some spare time. They are priorities.

CAN WE LOVE OTHERS MORE THAN WE LOVE OURSELVES?

The idea of self-love and self-acceptance was, and still is, revolutionary thinking for me. So in early 2009, I asked my blog readers what they thought about the importance of self-love and the idea that we can't love others more than we love ourselves. Well, there was quite the emotional debate in the comments section.

Several folks passionately disagreed with the notion of self-love being a requirement for loving others. Others argued that we can actually learn how to love ourselves more by loving others. Some folks just left comments like, "Thanks for ruining my day—I don't want to think about this."

There were two comments that addressed the complexity of these ideas in very straightforward terms. I'd like to share these with you. Justin Valentin, a mental health professional, writer, and photographer, wrote:

> Through my children I have learned to really love unconditionally, to be compassionate at times when I am feeling horrible, and to be so much more giving. When I look at my one daughter who looks so much like me, I can see myself as a little girl. This reminds me to be kinder to the little girl that lives inside me and to love and accept her as my own. It is the love for my girls that makes me want to be a better person and to work on loving and accepting myself. However, with that being said, it is still so much easier to love my daughters. . . .
>
> Perhaps thinking about it this way makes more sense: Many of my patients are mothers who struggle with drug addiction. They love their children more than themselves. They destroy their lives, hate themselves, and often damage their bodies beyond repair. They say they hate themselves, but they love their chil-

dren. They believe their children are lovable, but they believe they are unlovable. On the surface, one might say, yes, some of them love their children more than themselves. However, does loving your children mean that you are not intentionally poisoning them the way you poison yourself? Perhaps our issues are like secondhand smoke. At first, it was thought to be not so dangerous and by smoking we were *only hurting ourselves*. Yet [we have] come to find out, years later, secondhand smoke can be very deadly.[2]

Renae Cobb, a therapist by day and an undercover writer and occasional blog contributor by night, wrote:

Certainly, the people we love inspire us to heights of love and compassion that we might have never achieved otherwise, but to really scale those heights, we often have to go to the depths of who we are, light/shadow, good/evil, loving/destructive, and figure out our own stuff in order to love them better. So I'm not sure it's an either/or but a both/and. We love others fiercely, maybe more than we think we love ourselves, but that fierce love should drive us to the depths of our selves so that we can learn to be compassionate with ourselves.[3]

I agree with Justin and Renae. Loving and accepting ourselves are the ultimate acts of courage. In a society that says, "Put yourself last," self-love and self-acceptance are almost revolutionary.

If we want to take part in this revolution, we have to understand the anatomy of love and belonging; we need to understand when and why we hustle for worthiness rather than claim it; and we have to understand *the things that get in the way*. We encounter obstacles on every journey we make; the wholehearted journey is no different. In the next chapter we'll explore what I've found to be the greatest barriers to living and loving with our whole hearts.

The Things That
Get in the Way

In 2008, I was invited to give a talk at a very special event called The UP Experience. I really like the couple sponsoring the event, so without giving it much thought, I excitedly agreed to do it.

Well, you know how things always sound better when they're far away and you don't know the details? This was one of those things.

I accepted the invitation in late 2008 and never thought about it again until 2009, when the list of speakers was published on The UP Experience Web site. Suffice it to say that it was an overwhelmingly prestigious list of folks. And me. The event was billed as "16 of the world's most exciting thought-leaders and speakers. One mind-opening day!"

I freaked out. I couldn't imagine sharing the stage with Robert Ballard (the archaeological oceanographer who located the *Titanic*), Gavin Newsom (the mayor of San Francisco), Neil deGrasse Tyson (the astrophysicist who hosts NOVA and runs the Hayden Planetarium), and David Plouffe (the genius behind Obama's presidential campaign). And that's just four out of the fifteen.

On top of trying to manage feeling like a complete imposter, I was terrified about the format. The event was modeled after the TED talks (www.ted.com), and each speaker would have only twenty minutes to share their most innovative ideas with what they were calling a C-suite audience—an audience of mostly CEOs, CFOs, COOs, and CIOs who were paying $1,000 for the day-long event.

Seconds after I saw the list of speakers, I called my friend Jen and read the list of names to her. After the last name, I took a deep breath and said, "I'm not so sure about this."

Even though we were on the phone and she was thousands of miles away, I could see her shaking her head. "Put your measuring stick away, Brené."

I bristled. "What do you mean?"

Jen said, "I know you. You're already thinking about how to make your twenty-minute talk super 'researchy' and complicated."

I still didn't get it. "Well, yes. Of course I'm going to be researchy. Do you see this list of people? They're . . . they're . . . grown-ups."

Jen chuckled. "Do you need an age-check?"

Dead silence on my end.

Jen explained, "Here's the thing. You are a researcher, but your best work isn't from the head; it's talking from the heart. You'll be fine if you do what you do best—tell stories. Keep it real. Keep it honest."

I hung up, rolled my eyes, and thought: *Tell stories. You've got to be kidding? Maybe I could do a little puppet show too.*

Normally it takes me a day or two to develop a talk. I never speak from notes, but I normally have a visual presentation and an idea of what I want to say. Not this time. A puppet show would have been easier. I was paralyzed for weeks over this presentation. Nothing was working.

One evening, about two weeks before the event, Steve asked, "How's your UP talk coming along?"

I burst into tears. "It's not coming along. I don't have shit. I can't do it. I'm going to have to fake a car wreck or something."

Steve sat down next to me and grabbed my hand. "What's going on? This isn't like you. I've never seen you unravel like this over a talk. You do these things all the time."

I buried my head in my hands and mumbled, "I'm blocked. I just can't stop thinking about this horrible experience that happened several years ago."

Steve sounded surprised. "What experience?"

"I never told you about it," I explained. He leaned toward me and waited.

"Five years ago I bombed a talk like I had never bombed before or since. It was a total disaster, and I'm so afraid that it's going to happen again."

Steve couldn't believe that I had never told him about my disastrous experience. "What in the hell happened? Why didn't you tell me?"

I got up from the table and said, "I don't want to talk about it. It will just make it worse."

He grabbed my hand and pulled me back to the table. He looked at me in an I've-been-waiting-my-whole-life-to-use-your-line-against-you way. "Don't we need to talk about the hard things? Doesn't talking always make it better?" I was too tired to fight, so I told him this story.

Five years ago, when my first book came out, I was asked to speak at a women's networking lunch. I was so excited because, like The UP Experience, I would be speaking to a group of "normal" people—not therapists or academics, but normal businesspeople. In fact, this event was my first normal audience group.

I arrived early at the swanky country club where the event was being hosted, and I introduced myself to the woman in charge. After sizing me up for what felt like an eternity, she greeted me with a stack of short pronouncements. "Hello. You don't look like a researcher. I'm going to introduce you. I need your bio."

It was an uptight twist on "nice to meet you too," but okay. I handed her my bio and that was the beginning of the end.

She read it for thirty seconds before she gasped, turned to me, and, peering over her reading glasses, snapped, "This says that you're a shame researcher. Is that true?"

All of a sudden, I was ten years old and in the principal's office. I hung my head and whispered, "Yes, ma'am. I'm a shame researcher."

With her lips pursed, she popped, "Do. You. Study. Anything. Else?"

I couldn't tell her.

"*Do. You?*" she demanded.

"Yes. I also study fear and vulnerability."

She shrasped, which is like a combo shriek and gasp. "I was told that you collected research on how to be more joyful and how to have more connection and meaning in our lives."

Ah . . . got it. She didn't know anything about me. She must have heard about me from someone who failed to mention the nature of my work. Now it all made sense.

I tried to explain, "I don't really study 'how to be joyful' and have more meaning in our lives. I know a lot about these topics because I study the things that get in the way of joy, meaning, and connection." Without even responding to me, she walked out of the room and left me standing there.

Oh, the irony of a shame researcher standing in a puddle of "I'm not good enough."

She came back a few minutes later, looked right over the top of my head, and said, "Here's how this is going to go:

NUMBER 1: You're not going to talk about the things that get in the way. You're going to talk about the how-to part. That's what people want to hear. People want how-to.

NUMBER 2: Do not mention the word *shame*. People will be eating.

NUMBER 3: People want to be comfortable and joyful. That's all. Keep it joyful and comfortable."

I just stood there in total shock. After a few quiet seconds, she asked, "Okay?" and before I could say anything, she answered for me, "Sounds good."

Then, just as she started walking away, she turned around and said, "Light and breezy. People like light and breezy."

And, just in case I wasn't clear, she spread her fingers far apart and made huge sweeping gestures with her hands to illustrate "light" and "breezy" (picture Margaret Thatcher imitating Bob Fosse).

For forty minutes I stood in front of this group, totally paralyzed and repeating different versions of, "Joy is good. Happy is so, so good. We should all be joyful. And have meaning. Because they're just so darn good."

The women in the audience just smiled, nodded, and ate their chicken. It was a train wreck.

By the time I ended the story, Steve's face was all scrunched up and he was shaking his head. He's not a big fan of public speaking, so I think he was staving off his own anxiety as he listened to my disaster story.

But, strangely enough, telling the story made me less anxious. In fact, the second that I finished telling Steve the story, I felt different. I finally got it. My work—me—the decade I've spent doing research—it's all about "the things that get in the way." I'm not about the "how-to" because in ten years, I've never seen any evidence of "how-to" working without talking about the things that get in the way.

In a very powerful way, owning this story allowed me to claim who I am as a researcher and to establish my voice. I looked at Steve and smiled. "I don't do how-to."

For the first time in years, I realized that the country club woman wasn't out to get me and sabotage my talk. If that were the case, her ridiculous parameters wouldn't have been so devastating to me. Her list was symptomatic of our cultural fears. We don't want to be uncomfortable. We want a quick and dirty "how-to" list for happiness.

I don't fit that bill. Never have. Don't get me wrong, I'd love to skip over the hard stuff, but it just doesn't work. We don't change, we don't grow, and we don't move forward without the work. If we really want to live a joyful, connected, and meaningful life, we *must* talk about things that get in the way.

Until I owned and spoke this story, I let my lack of "quick tips" and "five simple steps" get in the way of my professional worthiness. Now that I've claimed that story, I see that my understanding of the darkness gives my search for the light context and meaning.

I'm happy to report that The UP Experience went really well. I actually told this "Light and Breezy" story as my talk. It was a risk, but I figured that even C-suites struggle with worthiness. A couple of weeks after the event, I got a call from the organizer. She said, "Congratulations! The evaluations are in and your talk finished in the top two of the day, and given what you study, you were the dark horse going in."

Here's the bottom line:

> If we want to live and love with our whole hearts, and if we want to engage with the world from a place of worthiness, we have to talk about the things that get in the way—especially shame, fear, and our resistance to vulnerability.

In Jungian circles, shame is often referred to as the swampland of the soul. I'm not suggesting that we wade out into the swamp and set up camp. I've done that and I can tell you that the swampland of the soul is an important place to visit, but you would *not* want to live there.

What I'm proposing is that we learn how to wade through it. We need to see that standing on the shore and catastrophizing about what could happen if we talked honestly about our fears is actually more painful than grabbing the hand of a trusted companion and crossing the swamp. And, most important, we need to learn why constantly trying to maintain our footing on the shifting shore as we gaze across to the other side of the swamp—where our worthiness waits for us—is much harder work than trudging across.

"How-to" is a seductive shortcut, and I understand that. Why cross the swamp if you can just bypass it?

But here's the dilemma: Why is "how-to" so alluring when, truthfully, we already know "how to" yet we're still standing in the same place longing for more joy, connection, and meaning?

Most everyone reading this book knows how to eat healthy. I can tell you the WeightWatcher points for every food in the grocery store. I can recite the South Beach Phase I grocery shopping list and I can tell you how many carbs are in 254 variations of cheese. We know how to eat healthy.

We also know how to make good choices with our money. We know how to take care of our emotional needs. We know all of this, yet we're facing what feel like insurmountable crises around addiction, debt, mental and physical health, violence, and loneliness—just to name a few.

Why? We have more access to information, more books, and more good science—why are we struggling like never before?

Because we don't talk about the things that get in the way of doing what we know is best for us, our children, our families, our organizations, and our communities.

I can know everything there is to know about eating healthy, but if it's one of those days when Ellen is struggling with a school project and Charlie's home sick from school and I'm trying to make a writing deadline and there's yet another school shooting and our grass is dying and my jeans don't fit and the economy is tanking and the Internet is down and we're out of poop bags for the dog—forget it! All I want to do is snuff out the sizzling anxiety with a pumpkin muffin, a bag of chips, and chocolate.

We don't talk about what keeps us eating until we're sick, busy beyond human scale, desperate to numb and take the edge off, and full of so much anxiety and self-doubt that we can't act on what we *know* is best for us. We don't talk about the hustle for worthiness that's become such a part of our lives that we don't even realize that we're dancing.

When I'm having one of those days that I just described, some of the anxiety is just a part of living, but there are days when most of my anxiety grows out of the expectations I put on myself. I want Ellen's project to be amazing. I want to take care of Charlie without worrying about my own deadlines. I want to take to the streets and scream in protest until schools no longer need to have monthly active-shooter drills. I want to show the world how great I am at balancing my family and career. I want our yard to look beautiful. I want people to see us picking up our dog's poop in biodegradable bags and think, *My God! They are such outstanding citizens.* There are days when I can fight the urge to be everything to everyone, and there are days when it gets the best of me.

As we discussed in the last chapter, when we struggle to believe in our worthiness, we hustle for it. The hustle for wor-

thiness has its own soundtrack and, for those of you who are
my age and older, it's not the funky "Do the Hustle" from the
'70s. It's the cacophony of shame tapes and gremlins—those
messages that fuel "never good enough."

- "What will people think?"
- "You can't *really* love yourself yet. You're not
  _____ enough." (pretty, skinny, suc-
  cessful, rich, talented, happy, smart, feminine, masculine, productive, nice, strong, tough, caring,
  popular, creative, well-liked, admired, contributing)
- "No one can find out about _____."
- "I'm going to pretend that everything is okay."
- "I can change to fit in if I have to!"
- "Who do you think you are to put your thoughts/art/
  ideas/beliefs/writing out in the world?"
- "Taking care of them is more important than taking
  care of me."
- "Don't take a stand on this issue—the vitriol will take
  you down. You're not strong enough."

Shame is that warm feeling that washes over us, making
us feel small, flawed, and never good enough. If we want to
develop shame resilience—the ability to recognize shame and
move through it while maintaining our worthiness and
authenticity—then we have to talk about why shame happens.

Honest conversations about shame can change the way we
live, love, parent, work, and build relationships. We have
thousands of letters and emails from readers that all say the

same thing: "I can't believe how much just naming and talking about shame changed my life!"

SHAME RESILIENCE 101

Here are the first three things that you need to know about shame:

1. We all have it. Shame is universal and one of the most primitive human emotions that we experience. The only people who don't experience shame lack the capacity for empathy and human connection.

2. We're all afraid to talk about shame.

3. The less we talk about shame, the more control it has over our lives.

Shame is basically the fear of being unlovable—it's the total opposite of owning our story and feeling worthy. In fact, the definition of shame that I developed from my research is:

> Shame is the intensely painful feeling or experience of believing that we are flawed and therefore unworthy of love, belonging, and connection.[1]

Shame keeps worthiness away by convincing us that owning our stories will lead to people thinking less of us. Shame is all about fear. We're afraid that people won't like us if they know the truth about who we are, where we come from, what we believe, how much we're struggling, or, believe it or not, how wonderful we are when soaring (sometimes it's just as hard to own our strengths as our struggles).

People often want to believe that shame is reserved for the folks who have survived terrible traumas, but this is not true. Shame is something we all experience. And while it feels as if shame hides in our darkest corners, it actually tends to lurk in all of the familiar places, including appearance and body image, family, parenting, money and work, health, addiction, sex, aging, and religion. To feel shame is to be human.

The stories of our struggles are difficult for everyone to own, and if we've worked hard to make sure everything looks "just right" on the outside, the stakes are high when it comes to truth-telling. This is why shame loves perfectionists—it's so easy to keep us quiet.

In addition to the fear of disappointing people or pushing them away with our stories, we're also afraid that if we tell our stories, the weight of a single experience will collapse upon us. There is a real fear that we can be buried or defined by an experience that, in reality, is only a sliver of who we are.

One example that comes to mind is one of the first interviews I did on shame. It's the story of a woman who worked up the courage to tell her neighbor that she was a recovering alcoholic, only to have her neighbor say, "I'm not sure I'm comfortable with my kids playing at your house anymore." This brave woman told me that she pushed through her fear and said, "But they've played here for two years, and I've been sober for twenty years. I'm not any different than I was ten minutes ago. Why are you?"

If shame is the universal fear of being unworthy of love and belonging, and if all people have an irreducible and innate need to experience love and belonging, it's easy to see why shame is often referred to as "the master emotion." We don't have to experience shame to be paralyzed by it—the fear of being perceived as unworthy is enough to force us to silence our stories.

And if we all have shame, the good news is that we're all capable of developing shame resilience. Shame resilience is the ability to recognize shame, to move through it constructively while maintaining worthiness and authenticity, and to ultimately develop more courage, compassion, and connection as a result of our experience. The first thing we need to understand about shame resilience is that the less we talk about shame, the more we have it.

Shame needs three things to grow out of control in our lives: secrecy, silence, and judgment. When something shaming happens and we keep it locked up, it festers and grows. It consumes us. We need to share our experience. Shame happens between people, and it heals between people. If we can find someone who has earned the right to hear our story, we need to tell it. Shame loses power when it is spoken. In this way, we need to cultivate our story to let go of shame, and we need to develop shame resilience in order to cultivate our story.

After a decade of research, I found that people with high levels of shame resilience share these four elements:

1.   They understand shame and recognize what messages and expectations trigger shame for them.

2.   They practice critical awareness by reality-checking the messages and expectations that tell us that *being imperfect* means being inadequate.

3.   They reach out and share their stories with people they trust.

4.   They speak shame—they use the word *shame,* they talk about how they're feeling, and they ask for what they need.

When I think about the participants in my study who spoke about the transformative power of story—the folks who own and share their stories—I realize that they are also people who practice shame resilience.

Because so much of worthiness and shame resilience is about owning our stories, I want to share one of my own shame-resilience stories with you. But before I do that, I want to address two commonly asked questions about shame. I think it will help you wrap your head and heart around this tough topic.

What's the difference between shame and guilt? The majority of shame researchers and clinicians agree that the difference between shame and guilt is best understood as the differences between "I am bad" and "I did something bad."

Guilt = I did something bad.
Shame = I am bad.

Shame is about who we are, and guilt is about our behaviors. We feel guilty when we hold up something we've done or failed to do against the kind of person we want to be. It's an uncomfortable feeling, but one that's helpful. When we apologize for something we've done, make amends to others, or change a behavior that we don't feel good about, guilt is most often the motivator. Guilt is just as powerful as shame, but its effect is often positive while shame often is destructive. When we see people apologize, make amends, or replace negative behaviors with more positive ones, guilt is often the motivator, not shame. In fact, in my research, I found that shame corrodes the part of us that believes we can change and do better.[2]

Doesn't shame keep us in line? Along with many other professionals, I've come to the conclusion that shame is much more likely to lead to destructive and hurtful behaviors than it is to be the solution. Again, it is human nature to want to feel worthy of love and belonging. When we experience shame, we feel disconnected and desperate for worthiness. Full of shame or the fear of shame, we are more likely to engage in self-destructive behaviors and to attack or shame others. In fact, shame is highly correlated with violence, aggression, depression, addiction, eating disorders, and bullying.

Children who use more shame self-talk (*I am bad*) versus guilt self-talk (*I did something bad*) struggle mightily with issues of self-worth and self-loathing. Using shame to parent teaches children that they are not inherently worthy of love.

SHAME RESEARCHER HEAL THYSELF!

No matter how much you know about shame, it can sneak up on you (trust me, I speak from experience).You can be in the middle of a shame experience without even knowing what's happening and why. The good news is that, with enough practice, shame resilience can also sneak up on you! The following story not only illustrates the insidious nature of shame, it also reinforces the importance of speaking about shame and telling our story.

For several months back in 2009, my relatively new blog was featured as an example site on the hosting company's main page. It was really fun because I got lots of traffic from people who wouldn't normally search out a blog on authenticity and courage. One day I got an email from a woman who liked my layout and design. I felt proud and grateful . . . until I got to this part of her email:

> I really like your blog. It's very creative and easy to read. The snap of you and your girlfriend in the theater would be the only exception . . . egads! I would never add a bad photo to a blog, but I am the photographer here. ;-)

I couldn't believe it. The photo she was referring to was a picture that I had taken of my good friend Laura and me sitting in a dark theater waiting for the *Sex and the City* movie to start. It was opening day and we were feeling goofy and excited, so I pulled out my phone and snapped a blurry, dark picture of us smiling in our theater seats.

I was so angry, confused, and shocked by this woman's comment about my picture, but I kept reading. She went on to ask a lot of questions about the blog's design and then closed her email by explaining that she works with many "clueless parents" and that she plans to let them know about my parenting work.

Whatever. I was so pissed off.

I paced back and forth in the kitchen, then sat down to pound out an email.

Draft #1 included this line: *"Egads! I would never put down someone's photography, but I'm the shame researcher here."*

Draft #2 included this line: *"I checked out your photography online. If you're concerned about posting bad photos, I'd rethink posting your photos."*

Draft #3 included this line: *"If you're going to send a shitty email, the least you can do is spell-check it. 'Their' does not mean 'they are.'"*

Mean. Nasty. I didn't care. But I also didn't send it. Something in my body stopped me. I read over my attack emails, took a deep breath, and then raced into the bedroom. I threw on my running shoes and a baseball cap and hit the pavement. I needed to get out of the house and discharge the weird energy coursing through my veins.

About one mile into my walk, I called my good friend Laura, the friend who happens to appear with me in said theater picture. I told her about the woman's email and she gasped, "Are you kidding me?"

"Nope. I'm not kidding. Wanna hear my three responses? I'm still trying to decide which one to use." I recited my "kill and destroy" responses, and she gasped again.

"Brené, those are really ballsy. I couldn't do it. I'd just be really hurt and probably cry." Laura and I talk about heavy stuff all of the time. We have a very comfortable rhythm. We can ping words all over the place or both get really quiet. We're always analyzing and saying things like "Okay, stay with me . . . I'm thinking . . ." and "Does this make sense?" or "*No. No.* Wait. It's coming to me."

At this point in our conversation, I said, "Laura, don't say anything. I need to think about what you just said." For two or three minutes the only sound was my sweaty panting.

Finally, I said, "You would get your feelings hurt and cry?"

Laura reluctantly responded, "Yes. Why?"

"Well . . ." I hesitated. "I'm thinking that crying and getting my feelings hurt would be the brave option for me."

Laura sounded surprised. "What do you mean?"

I explained the best I could. "Mean and nasty is my default setting. It doesn't take courage for me to be shaming back. I can use my shame superpowers for evil in a split second. Letting myself feel hurt—that's a totally different story. I think your default is my courage."

We talked about it for a while and decided that Laura's courage is acknowledging hurt without running from it, and my courage is acknowledging hurt and not hurting back. We also agreed that cruelty is never brave—it's mostly cheap and easy—especially in today's culture.

After talking for another mile or so, Laura asked, "Okay, now that we've got the acknowledging-hurt thing down, what would be the courageous thing for you to do with this email?"

I fought back tears. "Be hurt. Cry. Tell you about it. Let it go. Delete the email. Don't even respond."

Laura was quiet for a minute; then she blurted out, "Oh my God! That's shame resilience, right? You're practicing courage."

I was confused, like I had never heard the term before. "Huh? What do you mean?"

Laura patiently said, "Shame resilience—you know—your book? The blue one. The four elements of shame resilience: Name it. Talk about it. Own your story. Tell the story. Your book." We both started laughing. I thought to myself, *Holy crap. It works.*

A week later I was standing in front of a group of seventy graduate students who were taking my course on shame and empathy. I was talking about the four elements of shame resilience when one of the students raised her hand and asked for an example. I decided to tell the "egads" story. It's such a great example of how shame can happen at a totally unconscious level and how important it is to name it and talk about it.

I set up the story by describing my blog and my new commitment to learn photography. I told them that I felt vulnerable about sharing my pictures, and I felt ashamed and belittled when I received this critical email.

When I told them about my deep desire to respond with cruelty, several of the students buried their heads in their hands and others just looked away. I'm sure some were disappointed by my lack of enlightenment. Others looked plain scared.

One student raised his hand and said, "Can I ask a personal question?" Given that I was in the middle of sharing a vulnerable shame story, I figured that it couldn't hurt. I was wrong.

He bravely said, "I hear you saying that it was about feeling criticized about your photography, but was that really the vulnerability? Did the shame come from feeling like you were being criticized for a bad picture, or were you ashamed because you're allowing yourself to be vulnerable and open rather than closed and protected, and someone hurt you? Was it really about letting yourself be open to connection and getting hurt?"

My mouth got dry. I started sweating. I rubbed my forehead and then looked straight at the red-faced students.

"I can't believe it! That's exactly what happened. I didn't know it until this minute, but that's what happened. That's exactly what happened. I took a goofy picture in the theater—something I don't normally do, but I was with a close friend and we were feeling giddy and excited. I posted it online because I was excited and thought it was fun. Then someone criticized me."

A couple of the students glared at their brave colleague like, *Way to go. You traumatized her.* But I didn't feel traumatized. Or found out. Or exposed. I felt liberated. The story I needed to own in order to access my worthiness was not a story of a rookie photographer struggling with criticism over a photograph. It was the story of a pretty serious person being fun and spontaneous and goofy and imperfect and having someone poke at that vulnerability.

Resilience is often a slow unfolding of understanding. What did that experience mean to me? What were the gremlins mumbling? Not only do we need to own our story and love ourselves in the process, we have to figure out the real story! We also have to learn how we protect ourselves from shame if we want to develop worthiness.

WHAT DOES SHAME LOOK LIKE?

When it comes to understanding how we defend ourselves against shame, I have the utmost respect for the work from the Stone Center at Wellesley. Dr. Linda Hartling, a former relational-cultural theorist at the Stone Center and now the director of Human Dignity and Humiliation Studies, uses the late Karen Horney's work on moving toward, moving against, and moving away to outline the strategies of disconnection we use to deal with shame.[3]

According to Dr. Hartling, in order to deal with shame, some of us *move away* by withdrawing, hiding, silencing ourselves, and keeping secrets. Some of us *move toward* by seeking to appease and please. And some of us *move against* by trying to gain power over others, by being aggressive, and by using shame to fight shame (like sending really mean emails).

Most of us use all of these—at different times with different folks for different reasons. Yet all of these strategies move us away from our story. Shame is about fear, blame, and disconnection. Story is about worthiness and embracing the imperfections that bring us courage, compassion, and connection. If we want to live fully, without the constant fear of not being enough, we have to own our story. We also have to respond to shame in a way that doesn't exacerbate our shame. One way to do that is to recognize when we're in shame so we can react with intention.

Shame is a full-contact emotion. People with high levels of shame resilience know when shame is happening. The easiest way to know shame is to cultivate an awareness of our physical shame symptoms. As I mentioned in the chapter on courage, compassion, and connection, I know that I'm struggling with shame when that warm wash of inadequacy comes over me, my heart races, my face feels hot, my mouth gets dry, my armpits tingle, and time slows down. It's important to know our personal symptoms so we can get *deliberate* in our response to shame.

When we're in shame, we're not fit for human consumption. We need to get back on our emotional feet before we do, say, email, or text something that we'll regret. I know that it will take me ten to fifteen minutes to pull myself together and that I will definitely cry before I'm ready. I'll also need to pray. Knowing this is such a gift.

If you want to kick-start your shame resilience and story-claiming, start with these questions. Figuring out the answers can change your life:

1. Who do you become when you're backed into that shame corner?

2. How do you protect yourself?

3. Who do you call to work through the mean-nasties
   or the cry 'n' hides or the people-pleasing?

4. What's the most courageous thing you could do
   for yourself when you feel small and hurt?

Our stories are not meant for everyone. Hearing them is a privilege, and we should always ask ourselves this before we share: "Who has earned the right to hear my story?" If we have one or two people in our lives who can sit with us and hold space for our shame stories, and love us for our strengths and struggles, we are incredibly lucky. If we have a friend, or a small group of friends, or family who embraces our imperfections, vulnerabilities, and power, and fills us with a sense of belonging, we are incredible lucky.

We don't need love and belonging and story-catching from everyone in our lives, but we need it from at least one person. If we have that one person or that small group of confidants, the best way to acknowledge these connections is to acknowledge our worthiness. If we're working toward relationships based in love, belonging, and story, we have to start in the same place: I am worthy.

Cultivating Authenticity: Letting Go of What People Think

Often people attempt to live their lives backwards: they try to have more things, or more money, in order to do more of what they want so that they will be happier. The way it actually works is the reverse. You must first be who you really are, then do what you really need to do, in order to have what you want.

—MARGARET YOUNG

Before I started doing my research, I always thought of people as being either authentic or inauthentic. Authenticity was simply a quality that you had or that you were lacking. I think that's the way most of us use the term: "She's a very authentic person." But as I started immersing myself in the research and doing my own personal work, I realized that, like many desirable ways of being, authenticity is not something we have or don't have. It's a practice—a conscious choice of how we want to live.

Authenticity is a collection of choices that we have to make every day. It's about the choice to show up and be real. The choice to be honest. The choice to let our true selves be seen.

There are people who consciously practice being authentic, there are people who don't, and there are the rest of us who are authentic on some days and not so authentic on other days. Trust me, even though I know plenty about authenticity and it's something I work toward, if I am full of self-doubt or shame, I can sell myself out and be anybody you need me to be.

The idea that we can choose authenticity makes most of us feel both hopeful and exhausted. We feel hopeful because being real is something we value. Most of us are drawn to warm, down-to-earth, honest people, and we aspire to be like that in our own lives. We feel exhausted because without even giving it too much thought, most of us know that choosing authenticity in a culture that dictates everything from how much we're supposed to weigh to what our houses are supposed to look like is a huge undertaking.

Given the magnitude of the task at hand—be authentic in a culture that wants you to "fit in" and "people-please"—I decided to use my research to develop a definition of authenticity that I could use as a touchstone. What is the anatomy of authenticity? What are the parts that come together to create an authentic self? Here's what I developed:

Authenticity is the daily practice of letting go of who we think we're supposed to be and embracing who we are.

Choosing authenticity means

- cultivating the courage to be imperfect, to set boundaries, and to allow ourselves to be vulnerable;
- exercising the compassion that comes from knowing that we are all made of strength and struggle; and
- nurturing the connection and sense of belonging that can only happen when we believe that we are enough.

Authenticity demands wholehearted living and loving—even when it's hard, even when we're wrestling with the shame and fear of not being good enough, and especially when the joy is so intense that we're afraid to let ourselves feel it.

Mindfully practicing authenticity during our most soul-searching struggles is how we invite grace, gratitude, and joy into our lives.

You'll notice that many of the topics from the ten guideposts are woven throughout the definition. That theme will repeat itself throughout this book. All of the guideposts are interconnected and related to each other. My goal is to talk about them individually and collectively. I want us to explore how each of them works on its own and how they fit together. We'll spend the rest of the book unpacking terms like *perfec-*

tion so that we can understand why they're so important and what often gets in our way of living a wholehearted life.

Choosing authenticity is not an easy choice. E. E. Cummings wrote, "To be nobody-but-yourself in a world which is doing its best, night and day, to make you everybody but yourself—means to fight the hardest battle which any human being can fight—and never stop fighting." "Staying real" is one of the most courageous battles that we'll ever fight.

When we choose to be true to ourselves, the people around us will struggle to make sense of how and why we are changing. Partners and children might feel fearful and unsure about the changes they're seeing. Friends and family may worry about how our authenticity practice will affect them and our relationships with them. Some will find inspiration in our new commitment; others may perceive that we're changing too much—maybe even abandoning them or holding up an uncomfortable mirror.

It's not so much the *act of authenticity* that challenges the status quo—I think of it as the *audacity of authenticity*. Most of us have shame triggers around being perceived as self-indulgent or self-focused. We don't want our authenticity to be perceived as selfish or narcissistic. When I first started mindfully practicing authenticity and worthiness, I felt like every day was a walk through a gauntlet of gremlins. Their voices can be loud and unrelenting:

- "What if I think I'm enough, but others don't?"
- "What if I let my imperfect self be seen and known, and nobody likes what they see?"
- "What if my friends/family/co-workers like the per-

fect me better . . . you know, the one who takes care
of everything and everyone?"

Sometimes, when we push the system, it pushes back. The
pushback can be everything from eye rolls and whispers to
relationship struggles and feelings of isolation. There can also
be cruel and shaming responses to our authentic voices. In
my research on authenticity and shame, I found that speaking out is a major shame trigger for women and people who
are striving to meet cultural norms around femininity. Here's
how the research participants described the struggle to be authentic:

- Don't make people feel uncomfortable but be honest.
- Don't upset anyone or hurt anyone's feelings but say
  what's on your mind.
- Sound informed and educated but not like a know-
  it-all.
- Don't say anything unpopular or controversial but
  have the courage to disagree with the crowd.

I also found that we struggle when our opinions, feelings,
and beliefs conflict with our culture's gender expectations.
For example, researchers found that the top attributes that
we associate with "being feminine" include thin, nice, and
modest.[1] That means if we want to play it totally safe, we have
to be willing to stay as small, quiet, and attractive as possible.

When looking at the attributes associated with masculinity, the researchers identified these as important: emotional

control, primacy of work, control over women, and pursuit of status.[2] That means if complying with masculine norms is important to us and we want to play it safe, we must stop feeling, start earning, and give up on meaningful connection.

The thing is . . . authenticity isn't always the safe option. Sometimes choosing being real over being liked is all about playing it unsafe. It means stepping out of our comfort zone. And trust me, as someone who has stepped out on many occasions, it's easy to get knocked around when you're wandering through new territory.

It's easy to attack and criticize someone while they are risk-taking—voicing an unpopular opinion or sharing a new creation with the world or trying something new that they haven't quite mastered. Cruelty is cheap, easy, and rampant. It's also chicken-shit. Especially when you attack and criticize anonymously—like technology allows so many people to do these days.

As we struggle to be authentic and brave, it's important to remember that cruelty always hurts, even if the criticisms are untrue. When we go against the grain and put ourselves and our work out in the world, some people will feel threatened and they will go after what hurts the most—our appearance, our lovability, and even our parenting.

The problem is that when we don't care at all what people think and we're immune to hurt, we're also ineffective at connecting. Courage is telling our story, not being immune to criticism. Staying vulnerable is a risk we have to take if we want to experience connection.

If you're like me, practicing authenticity can feel like a

daunting choice—there's risk involved in putting your true self out in the world. But I believe there's even more risk in hiding yourself and your gifts from the world. Our unexpressed ideas, opinions, and contributions don't just go away. They are likely to fester and eat away at our worthiness. I think we should be born with a warning label similar to the ones that come on cigarette packages: *Caution: If you trade in your authenticity for being liked, you may experience the following: anxiety, depression, eating disorders, addiction, rage, blame, resentment, and inexplicable grief.*

Sacrificing who we are for the sake of what other people think just isn't worth it. Yes, there can be authenticity growing pains for the people around us, but in the end, being true to ourselves is the best gift we can give the people we love. When I let go of trying to be everything to everyone, I had much more time, attention, love, and connection for the important people in my life. My authenticity practice can be hard on Steve and the kids—mostly because it requires time, energy, and attention. But the truth is that Steve, Ellen, and Charlie are engaged in the same struggle. We all are.

DIG DEEP

Get Deliberate: Find a mantra, word, or saying that grounds you! Whenever I'm faced with a vulnerable situation, I get deliberate with my intentions by repeating this to myself: "Don't shrink. Don't puff up. Stand on your sacred ground." Saying this little mantra helps me remember not to get small so other people are comfortable and not to throw up my armor as a way to protect myself.

Get Inspired: I'm inspired by everyone who shares their work and opinions with the world. Courage is contagious. My friend Katherine Center says, "You have to be brave with your life so that others can be brave with theirs."[3]

Get Going: I try to make authenticity my number one goal when I go into a situation where I'm feeling vulnerable. If authenticity is my goal and I keep it real, I never regret it. I might get my feelings hurt, but I rarely feel shame. When acceptance or approval becomes my goal, and it doesn't work out, that can trigger shame for me: "I'm not good enough." If the goal is authenticity and they don't like me, I might feel disappointment, frustration, or even grief, but I'm okay. If the goal is being liked and they don't like me, I'm in trouble. I get going by making authenticity the priority.

Cultivating Self-Compassion: Letting Go of Perfectionism

The thing that is really hard, and really amazing, is giving up on being perfect and beginning the work of becoming yourself.

—ANNA QUINDLEN[1]

One of the best parts of my work is receiving letters and emails from readers. In early 2009, I received my one thousandth email from a reader of *I Thought It Was Just Me*. To celebrate, I decided to facilitate an eight-week read-along of the book. I called it the *Shame.Less Joy.Full* read-along.

Just before the read-along started, I received an email that said, "I love the idea of a read-along. I don't think I have shame issues, but if you ever do something on perfectionism, I'll be the first in line." Her sign-off was followed by a short little sentence that read: "PS—shame and perfectionism aren't related, are they?"

I emailed her back and explained the relationship between shame and perfectionism: Where perfectionism exists, shame is always lurking. In fact, shame is the birthplace of perfectionism.

I loved her response: "You might want to talk about that before WE start the read-along. My friends and I know that we struggle with perfectionism, but we don't claim shame."

We don't claim shame. You can't believe how many times I've heard that! I know *shame* is a daunting word. The problem is that when we don't claim shame, it claims us. And one of the ways it sneaks into our lives is through perfectionism.

As a recovering perfectionist and an aspiring good-enoughist, I've found it extremely helpful to bust some of the myths about perfectionism so that we can develop a definition that accurately captures what it is and what it does to our lives.

- *Perfectionism is* not *the same thing as striving to be your best.* Perfectionism is *not* about healthy achievement and growth. Perfectionism is the belief that if we live perfect, look perfect, and act perfect, we can minimize or avoid the pain of blame, judgment, and shame. It's a shield. Perfectionism is a twenty-ton shield that we lug around thinking it will protect us when, in fact, it's the thing that's really preventing us from taking flight.
- *Perfectionism is* not *self-improvement.* Perfectionism is, at its core, about trying to earn approval and acceptance. Most perfectionists were raised being praised for achievement and performance (grades,

manners, rule-following, people-pleasing, appearance, sports). Somewhere along the way, we adopt
this dangerous and debilitating belief system: I am
what I accomplish and how well I accomplish it.
Please. Perform. Perfect. Healthy striving is self-
focused—*How can I improve?* Perfectionism is
other-focused—*What will they think?*

Understanding the difference between healthy striving
and perfectionism is critical to laying down the shield and
picking up your life. Research shows that perfectionism ham-
pers success. In fact, it's often the path to depression, anxiety,
addiction, and life-paralysis.[2] *Life-paralysis* refers to all of
the opportunities we miss because we're too afraid to put
anything out in the world that could be imperfect. It's also all
of the dreams that we don't follow because of our deep fear of
failing, making mistakes, and disappointing others. It's terrifying to risk when you're a perfectionist; your self-worth is on
the line.

I put these four insights together to craft a definition of
perfectionism (because you know how much I love to get
words wrapped around my struggles!). It's long, but man, has
it helped me!

- Perfectionism is a self-destructive and addictive belief system that fuels this primary thought: *If I look
  perfect, live perfect, work perfect, and do everything perfectly, I can avoid or minimize the painful
  feelings of shame, judgment, and blame.*

- Perfectionism is self-destructive simply because there is no such thing as perfect. Perfection is an unattainable goal. Additionally, perfectionism is more about perception—we want to be perceived as perfect. Again, this is unattainable—there is no way to control perception, regardless of how much time and energy we spend trying.

- Perfectionism is addictive because when we invariably do experience shame, judgment, and blame, we often believe it's because we weren't perfect enough. So rather than questioning the faulty logic of perfectionism, we become even more entrenched in our quest to live, look, and do everything just right.

- Feeling shamed, judged, and blamed (and the fear of these feelings) are realities of the human experience. Perfectionism actually increases the odds that we'll experience these painful emotions and often leads to self-blame: *It's my fault. I'm feeling this way because "I'm not good enough."*

To overcome perfectionism, we need to be able to acknowledge our vulnerabilities to the universal experiences of shame, judgment, and blame; develop shame resilience; and practice self-compassion. When we become more loving and compassionate with ourselves and we begin to practice shame resilience, we can embrace our imperfections. It is in the process of embracing our imperfections that we find our truest gifts: courage, compassion, and connection.

Based on my data, I don't think that some people are perfectionists and others are not. I think perfectionism exists along a continuum. We all have some perfectionistic tendencies. For some, perfectionism may only emerge when they're feeling particularly vulnerable. For others, perfectionism can be compulsive, chronic, and debilitating, similar to addiction.

I've started to work on my perfectionism, one messy piece at a time. In doing so, I finally understand (in my bones) the difference between perfectionism and healthy achieving. Exploring our fears and changing our self-talk are two critical steps in overcoming perfectionism.

Here's my example:

Like many people, I struggle with body image, self-confidence, and the always-complicated relationship between food and emotions. Here's the difference between perfectionism diets and healthy goals.

Perfectionism self-talk: "Ugh. Nothing fits. I'm fat and I look like shit. I'm ashamed of how I look. I need to be different than I am right now to be worthy of love and belonging."

Healthy-striving self-talk: "I want this for me. I want to feel better and be healthier. The scale doesn't dictate if I'm loved and accepted. If I believe that I'm worthy of love and respect now, I will invite courage, compassion, and connection into my life. I want to figure this out for me. I can do this."

For me, the results of this shift were life changing. Perfectionism didn't lead to results. It led to peanut butter.

I've also had to rely on the old "fake it 'til you make it" a few times. I think of it as practicing imperfection. For example, right after I started working on this definition, some friends dropped by our house. My then nine-year-old daughter, Ellen, shouted, "Mom! Don and Julie are at the door!" Our house was trashed, and I could tell by the sound of Ellen's voice that she was thinking, *Oh no! Mom's going to freak.*

I said, "Just a second," as I hurried to get dressed. She ran back to my room and said, "Do you want me to help pick up?"

I said, "No, I'm just getting dressed. I'm so glad they're here. What a nice surprise! Who cares about the house!" Then I put myself in a Serenity Prayer trance.

So, if we want to live and love with our whole hearts, how do we keep perfectionism from sabotaging our efforts? When I interviewed people who were engaging with the world from a place of authenticity and worthiness, I realized that they had a lot in common regarding perfectionism.

First, they spoke about their imperfections in a tender and honest way, and without shame and fear. Second, they were slow to judge themselves and others. They appeared to operate from a place of "We're all doing the best we can." Their courage, compassion, and connection seemed rooted in the way they treated themselves. I wasn't quite sure how to capture these attributes, but I assumed that they were separate qualities. That is until I found Dr. Kristin Neff's work on self-compassion. Let's explore the concept of self-compassion and why it's essential to practicing authenticity and embracing imperfection.

SELF-COMPASSION

A moment of self-compassion can change your
entire day. A string of such moments can change
the course of your life.

—CHRISTOPHER K. GERMER[3]

Dr. Kristin Neff is a researcher and professor at the University of Texas at Austin. She runs the Self-Compassion Research Lab, where she studies how we develop and practice self-compassion. According to Neff, self-compassion has three elements: self-kindness, common humanity, and mindfulness.[4] Here are abbreviated definitions for each of these:

- **SELF-KINDNESS:** Being warm and understanding toward ourselves when we suffer, fail, or feel inadequate, rather than ignoring our pain or flagellating ourselves with self-criticism.
- **COMMON HUMANITY:** Common humanity recognizes that suffering and feelings of personal inadequacy are part of the shared human experience—something we all go through rather than something that happens to "me" alone.
- **MINDFULNESS:** Taking a balanced approach to negative emotions so that feelings are neither suppressed nor exaggerated. We cannot ignore our pain and feel compassion for it at the same time. Mindfulness requires that we not "over-identify" with thoughts and feelings, so that we are caught up and swept away by negativity.

One of the many things that I love about Dr. Neff's work is her definition of *mindfulness*. Many of us think that being mindful means not avoiding painful emotions. Her definition reminds us that mindfulness also means not over-identifying with or exaggerating our feelings. I think that's key for those of us who struggle with perfectionism. I'll give you the "perfect" example: I recently emailed an author to ask if I could quote her work in this book. I included the exact passage that I wanted to include so that she could make an informed choice. She generously said yes, but warned me against using the paragraph in the email because I had misspelled her name.

I went into total perfection paralysis. "Oh my God! I'm writing to ask her if I can quote her and I misspell her name. She probably thinks I'm a total hack. Why was I so sloppy?" It wasn't a shame attack—I didn't get sucked under that far—but I also didn't respond with self-compassion. I came close to being "swept away by negative reactivity." Luckily, a draft of this chapter was on the table next to me. I looked down at it and smiled. *Be kind to yourself, Brené. This is not a big deal.*

Using this email exchange as an example, you can see how my perfectionism and lack of self-compassion could easily lead to judgment. I think of myself as a sloppy hack because of one tiny mistake. By the same token, when I get an email from someone and there are mistakes, I have a tendency to make sweeping judgments. It gets really dangerous if Ellen comes to me and says, "I just sent my teacher an email, and I accidentally misspelled her name." Do I say, "What? That's unacceptable!" or do I say, "I've done the same thing—mistakes happen."

Perfectionism never happens in a vacuum. It touches everyone around us. We pass it down to our children, we infect our workplace with impossible expectations, and it's suffocating for our friends and families. Thankfully, compassion also spreads quickly. When we're kind to ourselves, we create a reservoir of compassion that we can extend to others. Our children learn how to be self-compassionate by watching us, and the people around us feel free to be authentic and connected.

DIG DEEP

Get Deliberate: One tool that's helped me get deliberate about my self-compassion is Dr. Neff's Self-Compassion Scale.[5] It's a short test that measures the elements of self-compassion (self-kindness, common humanity, and mindfulness) and the things that get in the way (self-judgment, isolation, and overidentification). The scale helped me to realize that I do really well in terms of common humanity and mindfulness, but self-kindness needs my constant attention. The Self-Compassion Scale and other wonderful information are available on Dr. Neff's Web site: www.self-compassion .org.

Get Inspired: Most of us are trying to live an authentic life. Deep down, we want to take off our game face and be real and imperfect. There is a line from Leonard Cohen's song "Anthem" that serves as a reminder to me when I get into that place where I'm trying to control everything and make it perfect.[6] The line is, "There is a crack in everything. That's how the light gets in." So many of us run around spackling all of the cracks, trying to make everything look just right. This line helps me remember the beauty of the cracks (and the messy house and the imperfect manuscript and the too-tight jeans). It reminds me that our imperfections are not inadequacies; they are reminders that we're all in this together. Imperfectly, but together.

Get Going: Sometimes it helps me to wake up in the morning and tell myself, "Today, I'm going to believe that showing up is enough."

Cultivating a Resilient Spirit: Letting Go of Numbing and Powerlessness

She could never go back and make some of the details pretty. All she could do was move forward and make the whole beautiful.

—TERRI ST. CLOUD,
WWW.BONESIGHARTS.COM[1]

Resilience—the ability to overcome adversity—has been a growing topic of study since the early 1970s. In a world plagued by stress and struggle, everyone from psychologists, psychiatrists, and social workers to clergy and criminal justice researchers want to know why and how some folks are better at recovering from hardship than others. We want to understand why some people can cope with stress and trauma in a way that allows them to move forward in their lives, and why other people appear more affected and stuck.

As I collected and analyzed my data, I recognized that

many of the people I interviewed were describing stories of resilience. I heard stories about people cultivating whole-hearted lives despite adversity. I learned about people's ca-pacities to stay mindful and authentic under great stress and anxiety, and I heard people describe how they were able to transform trauma into wholehearted thriving.

It wasn't difficult to recognize these stories as tales of re-silience because I was in graduate school during the heyday of resilience research. I knew these narratives were threaded with what we call *protective factors*—the things we do, have, and practice that give us the bounce.

WHAT MAKES UP RESILIENCE?

If you look at the research, here are five of the most common factors of resilient people:

1. They are resourceful and have good problem-solving skills.

2. They are more likely to seek help.

3. They hold the belief that they can do something that will help them to manage their feelings and to cope.

4. They have social support available to them.

5. They are connected with others, such as family or friends.[2]

Of course, there are more factors, depending on the researchers, but these are the big ones.

At first, I hoped the patterns that I observed in my research would lead to a very straightforward conclusion—
resilience is a core component of wholeheartedness—just like
the other guideposts. But there was something more to what
I was hearing. The stories had more in common than just resilience; all of these stories were about spirit.

According to the people I interviewed, the very foundation
of the "protective factors"—the things that made them
bouncy—was their spirituality. By spirituality, I'm not talking
about religion or theology, but I am talking about a shared
and deeply held belief. Based on the interviews, here's how I
define *spirituality:*

> Spirituality is recognizing and celebrating that we
> are all inextricably connected to each other by a power
> greater than all of us, and that our connection to that
> power and to one another is grounded in love and com-
> passion. Practicing spirituality brings a sense of per-
> spective, meaning, and purpose to our lives.

Without exception, spirituality—the belief in connection,
a power greater than self, and interconnections grounded in
love and compassion—emerged as a component of resilience.
Most people spoke of God, but not everyone. Some were occasional churchgoers; others were not. Some worshipped at
fishing holes; others in temples, mosques, or at home. Some
struggled with the idea of religion; others were devout mem-

bers of organized religions. The one thing that they all had in common was spirituality as the foundation of their resilience.

From this foundation of spirituality, three other significant patterns emerged as being essential to resilience:

1. Cultivating hope

2. Practicing critical awareness

3. Letting go of numbing and taking the edge off vulnerability, discomfort, and pain

Let's take a look at each of these and how they're connected to resilience and spirit.

HOPE AND POWERLESSNESS

As a researcher, I can't think of two words that are more misunderstood than the words *hope* and *power*. As soon as I realized that hope is an important piece of wholehearted living, I started investigating and found the work of C. R. Snyder, a former researcher at the University of Kansas, Lawrence.[3] Like most people, I always thought of hope as an emotion— like a warm feeling of optimism and possibility. I was wrong.

I was shocked to discover that hope is *not* an emotion; it's a way of thinking or a cognitive process. Emotions play a supporting role, but hope is really a thought process made up of what Snyder calls a trilogy of goals, pathways, and agency.[4] In very simple terms, hope happens when

- We have the ability to set realistic goals *(I know where I want to go)*.
- We are able to figure out how to achieve those goals, including the ability to stay flexible and develop alternative routes *(I know how to get there, I'm persistent, and I can tolerate disappointment and try again)*.
- We believe in ourselves *(I can do this!)*.

So, hope is a combination of setting goals, having the tenacity and perseverance to pursue them, and believing in our own abilities.

And, if that's not news enough, here's something else: Hope is learned! Snyder suggests that we learn hopeful, goal-directed thinking in the context of other people. Children most often learn hope from their parents. Snyder says that to learn hopefulness, children need relationships that are characterized by boundaries, consistency, and support. I think it's so empowering to know that I have the ability to teach my children how to hope. It's not a crapshoot. It's a conscious choice.

To add to Snyder's work on hope, I found in my research that participants who self-report as hopeful put considerable value on persistence and hard work. The new cultural belief that everything should be *fun, fast, and easy* is inconsistent with hopeful thinking. It also sets us up for hopelessness. When we experience something that is difficult and requires significant time and effort, we are quick to think, *This is supposed to be easy; it's not worth the effort,* or, *This should be easier: it's only hard and slow because I'm not good at it.*

Hopeful self-talk sounds more like, *This is tough, but I can do it.*

On the other hand, for those of us who have the tendency to believe that everything worthwhile should involve pain and suffering (like yours truly), I've also learned that *never fun, fast, and easy* is as detrimental to hope as *always fun, fast, and easy.* Given my abilities to chase down a goal and bulldog it until it surrenders from pure exhaustion, I resented learning this. Before this research I believed that unless blood, sweat, and tears were involved, it must not be that important. I was wrong. Again.

We develop a hopeful mind-set when we understand that some worthy endeavors will be difficult and time consuming and not enjoyable at all. Hope also requires us to understand that just because the process of reaching a goal happens to be fun, fast, and easy doesn't mean that it has less value than a difficult goal. If we want to cultivate hopefulness, we have to be willing to be flexible and demonstrate perseverance. Not every goal will look and feel the same. Tolerance for disappointment, determination, and a belief in self are the heart of hope.

As a college professor and researcher, I spend a significant amount of time with teachers and school administrators. Over the past two years I've become increasingly concerned that we're raising children who have little tolerance for disappointment and that some, who come from various forms of privilege including race and class, have a strong sense of entitlement. Entitlement is very different than agency. Entitlement is "I deserve this just because I want it" and agency is "I know I can do this." The combination of fear of disappointment, entitlement, and performance pressure is a recipe for hopelessness and self-doubt.

Hopelessness is dangerous because it leads to feelings of powerlessness. Unlike the word *hope,* we often think of power as negative. It's not. The best definition of *power* comes from Martin Luther King Jr. He described power as the ability to achieve our purpose and to effect change. If we question our need for power, think about this: *How do you feel when you believe that you are powerless to change something in your life?*

Powerlessness is dangerous. For most of us, the inability to effect change is a desperate feeling. We need resilience and hope and a spirit that can carry us through the doubt and fear. We need to believe that we can effect change if we want to live and love with our whole hearts.

PRACTICING CRITICAL AWARENESS

Practicing critical awareness is about reality-checking the messages and expectations that drive the "never good enough" gremlins. From the time we wake up to the time our head hits the pillow at night, we are bombarded with messages and expectations about every aspect of our lives. From magazine ads and TV commercials to movies and music, we're told exactly what we should look like, how much we should weigh, how often we should have sex, how we should parent, how we should decorate our houses, and which car we should drive. It's absolutely overwhelming, and, in my opinion, no one is immune. Trying to avoid media messages is like holding your breath to avoid air pollution—it's not going to happen.

It's in our biology to trust what we see with our eyes. This makes living in a carefully edited, overproduced, and Photo-shopped world very dangerous. If we want to cultivate a resilient spirit and stop falling prey to comparing our ordinary lives with manufactured images, we need to know how to reality-check what we see. We need to be able to ask and answer these questions:

1. Is what I'm seeing real? Do these images convey real life or fantasy?

2. Do these images reflect healthy, wholehearted living, or do they turn my life, my body, my family, and my relationships into objects and commodities?

3. Who benefits by my seeing these images and feeling bad about myself? *Hint: This is ALWAYS about money and/or control.*

In addition to being essential to resilience, practicing critical awareness is actually one of the four elements of shame resilience. Shame works like the zoom lens on a camera. When we are feeling shame, the camera is zoomed in tight and all we see is our flawed selves, alone and struggling. We think to ourselves, *I'm the only one with a muffin-top? Am I the only one with a family who is messy, loud, and out of control? Am I the only one not having sex 4.3 times per week? Something is wrong with me. I am alone.*

When we zoom out, we start to see a completely different picture. We see many people in the same struggle. Rather than thinking, *I'm the only one,* we start thinking, *I can't believe it! You too? I'm normal? I thought it was just me!* Once we start to see the big picture, we are better able to reality-check our shame triggers and the messages and expectations that we're never good enough.

As I mentioned earlier, practicing spirituality brings perspective, meaning, and purpose to our lives. When we allow ourselves to become culturally conditioned to believe that we are not enough and that we don't make enough or have enough, it damages our soul. This is why I think practicing critical awareness and reality-checking is as much about spirituality as it is about critical thinking.

NUMBING AND TAKING THE EDGE OFF

I talked to many research participants who were struggling with worthiness. When we talked about how they dealt with difficult emotions (such as shame, grief, fear, despair, disappointment, and sadness), I heard over and over about the need to numb and take the edge off of feelings that cause vulnerability, discomfort, and pain. Participants described engaging in behaviors that numbed their feelings or helped them to avoid experiencing pain. Some of these participants were fully aware that their behaviors had a numbing effect, while others did not seem to make that connection. When I interviewed the participants whom I'd describe as living a wholehearted life about the same topic, they consistently talked about *trying to feel the feelings, staying mindful about numbing behaviors, staying in it,* and *trying to lean into the discomfort of hard emotions.*

I knew this was a critically important finding in my research, so I spent several hundred interviews trying to better
understand the consequences of numbing and how taking the
edge off behaviors is related to addiction. Here's what I
learned:

1.   Most of us engage in behaviors (consciously or
not) that help us to numb and take the edge off vulnerability, pain, and discomfort.

2.   Addiction can be described as chronically and
compulsively numbing and taking the edge off of feelings.

3.   We cannot selectively numb emotions. When we
numb the painful emotions, we also numb the positive
emotions.

The most powerful emotions that we experience have very
sharp points, like the tip of a thorn. When they prick us, they
cause discomfort and even pain. Just the anticipation or fear
of these feelings can trigger intolerable vulnerability in us.
We know it's coming. For many of us, our first response to the
vulnerability and pain of these sharp points is not to lean into
the discomfort and feel our way through but rather to make it
go away. We do that by numbing and taking the edge off the
pain with whatever provides the quickest relief. We can anes-
thetize with a whole bunch of stuff, including alcohol, drugs,
food, sex, relationships, money, work, caretaking, gambling,
staying busy, affairs, chaos, shopping, planning, perfectionism, constant change, and the Internet.

Before conducting this research I thought that numbing and taking the edge off was just about addiction, but I don't believe that anymore. Now I believe that everyone numbs and takes the edge off and that addiction is about engaging in these behaviors compulsively and chronically. The people in my study whom I would describe as fully engaged in whole-hearted living were not immune to numbing. The primary difference seemed to be that they were aware of the dangers of numbing and had developed the ability to feel their way through high-vulnerability experiences.

I definitely believe that genetics and neurobiology can play a critical role in addiction, but I also believe that there are countless people out there struggling with numbing and taking the edge off because the disease model of addiction doesn't fit their experiences as closely as a model that takes numbing processes into consideration. Not everyone's addiction is the same.

When I first started my research, I was very familiar with addiction. If you follow my work, you probably know that I've been sober since 1996. I've always been very up front about my experience, but it wasn't until I started working through this research that I started to understand the core of my struggle.

Now I get it.

My confusion stemmed from the fact that I never have felt completely in sync with the recovery community. Abstinence and the Twelve Steps are powerful and profoundly important principles in my life, but not everything about the recovery movement fits for me. For example, millions of people owe their lives to the power that comes from saying, "Hi, I'm (name), and I'm an alcoholic." That's never fit for me. Even though I'm grateful for my sobriety, and I'm convinced that it has radically changed my life, saying those words has always felt disempowering and strangely disingenuous for me.

I have often wondered if I felt out of place because I quit so many things at one time. My first sponsor couldn't figure out what meeting I needed and was perplexed by my "very high bottom" (I quit drinking because I wanted to learn more about true self, and my wild party-girl persona kept getting in the way). She looked at me one night and said, "You have the pupu platter of addictions—a little bit of everything. To be safe, it would be best if you just quit drinking, smoking, comfort-eating, and getting in your family's business."

I remember looking at her, throwing my fork on the table, and saying, "Well, that's just awesome. I guess I'll have some free time on my hands for all of the meetings." I never found my meeting. I quit drinking and smoking the day after I finished my master's degree and made my way through enough meetings to work the Steps and get one year of sobriety under my belt.

Now I know why.

I've spent most of my life trying to outrun vulnerability and uncertainty. I wasn't raised with the skills and emotional practice needed to "lean into discomfort," so over time I basically became a take-the-edge-off-aholic. But they don't have meetings for that. And after some brief experimenting, I learned that describing your addiction that way in a meeting doesn't always go over very well with the purists.

For me, it wasn't just the dance halls, cold beer, and Marlboro Lights of my youth that got out of hand—it was banana bread, chips and queso, email, work, staying busy, incessant worrying, planning, perfectionism, and anything else that could dull those agonizing and anxiety-fueled feelings of vulnerability.

I've had a couple of friends respond to my "I'm a take-the-edge-off-aholic" with concern about their own habits: "I drink a couple of glasses of wine every night—is that bad?" "I always shop when I'm stressed or depressed." "I come out of my skin if I'm not always going and staying busy."

Again, after years of research, I'm convinced that we all numb and take the edge off. The question is, does our _____ (eating, drinking, spending, gambling, saving the world, incessant gossiping, perfectionism, sixty-hour workweek) get in the way of our authenticity? Does it stop us from being emotionally honest and setting boundaries and feeling like we're enough? Does it keep us from staying out of judgment and from feeling connected? Are we using _____ to hide or escape from the reality of our lives?

Understanding my behaviors and feelings through a vulnerability lens rather than strictly through an addiction lens changed my entire life. It also strengthened my commitment to sobriety, abstinence, health, and spirituality. I can definitely say, "Hi. My name is Brené, and today I'd like to deal with vulnerability and uncertainty with an apple fritter, a beer and cigarette, and spending seven hours on Instagram." That feels uncomfortably honest.

WHEN WE NUMB THE DARK,
WE NUMB THE LIGHT

In another very unexpected discovery, my research also taught me that there's no such thing as selective emotional numbing. There is a full spectrum of human emotions and when we numb the dark, we numb the light. While I was "taking the edge off" the pain and vulnerability, I was also unintentionally dulling my experiences of good feelings, like joy. Looking back, I can't imagine any research finding that has changed what my daily life looks like more than this. Now I can lean into joy, even when it makes me feel tender and vulnerable. In fact, I expect tender and vulnerable.

Joy is as thorny and sharp as any of the dark emotions. To love someone fiercely, to believe in something with your whole heart, to celebrate a fleeting moment in time, to fully engage in a life that doesn't come with guarantees—these are risks that involve vulnerability and often pain. When we lose our tolerance for discomfort, we lose joy. In fact, addiction research shows us that an intensely positive experience is as likely to cause relapse as an intensely painful experience.[5]

We can't make a list of all of the "bad" emotions and say, "I'm going to numb these" and then make a list of the positive emotions and say, "I'm going to fully engage in these!" You can imagine the vicious cycle this creates: I don't experience much joy so I have no reservoir to draw from when hard things happen. They feel even more painful, so I numb. I numb so I don't experience joy. And so on.

More on joy is coming in the next chapter. For now, as the sharp edges have started to come back in my own life, I'm learning that recognizing and leaning into the discomfort of vulnerability teaches us how to live with joy, gratitude, and grace. I'm also learning that the uncomfortable and scary leaning requires both spirit and resilience.

The most difficult thing about what I'm proposing in this chapter is captured by a question that I get a lot (especially from my colleagues in the academic world): Is spirituality a necessary component for resilience? The answer is *yes*.

Feelings of hopelessness, fear, blame, pain, discomfort, vulnerability, and disconnection sabotage resilience. The only experience that seems broad and fierce enough to combat a list like that is the belief that we're all in this together and that something greater than us has the capacity to bring love and compassion into our lives.

Again, I didn't find that any one interpretation of spirituality has the corner on the resilience market. It's not about denominations or dogma. Practicing spirituality is what brings healing and creates resilience. For me, spirituality is about connecting with God, and I do that most often through nature, community, and music. We all have to define spirituality in a way that inspires us.

Whether we're overcoming adversity, surviving trauma, or dealing with stress and anxiety, having a sense of purpose, meaning, and perspective in our lives allows us to develop understanding and move forward. Without purpose, meaning, and perspective, it is easy to lose hope, numb our emotions, or become overwhelmed by our circumstances. We feel reduced, less capable, and lost in the face of struggle. The heart of spirituality is connection. When we believe in that inextricable connection, we don't feel alone.

DIG DEEP

Get Deliberate: A good friend of mine heard this wonderful intention-setting reminder during a Twelve Step meeting. I love it! It's called the vowel check: AEIOUY.

A = Have I been **A**bstinent today? (However you define that—it's way more challenging to define abstinence when it comes to things like food, work, and the computer, but the process of defining what it means to you is worth the effort. It changed my life.)

E = Have I **E**xercised today?

I = What have **I** done for myself today?

O = What have I done for **O**thers today?

U = Am I holding on to **U**nexpressed emotions today?

Y = **Y**eah! What is something good that's happened today?

Get Inspired: I'm inspired by this quote from writer and re-searcher Elisabeth Kübler-Ross: "People are like stained-glass windows. They sparkle and shine when the sun is out, but when the darkness sets in, their beauty is revealed only if there is a light from within." I really do believe the light that I saw within the resilient people I interviewed was their spirit. I love the idea of being "lit from within."

Get Going: I love daily meditations and prayers. Sometimes the best way for me to get going is quiet prayer.

Cultivating Gratitude and Joy: Letting Go of Scarcity and Fear of the Dark

Earlier I mentioned how surprised I was to see certain concepts from my research emerge in pairs or groups. These "collections of concepts" have created major paradigm shifts for me in terms of the way I think about my life and the choices I make every day.

A good example of this is the way that love and belonging go together. Now I understand that in order to feel a true sense of belonging, I need to bring the real me to the table and that I can only do that if I'm practicing self-love. For years I thought it was the other way around: I'll do whatever it takes to fit in, I'll feel accepted, and that will make me like myself better. *(Just typing those words and thinking about how many years I spent living that way makes me weary. No wonder I was tired for so long!)*

In many ways, this research has not only taught me new ways to think about how I want to live and love, it's taught me about the relationship between my experiences and choices. One of the most profound changes in my life happened when I got my head around the relationship between gratitude and joy. I always thought that joyful people were grateful people. I mean, why wouldn't they be? They have all of that goodness to be grateful for. But after spending countless hours collecting stories about joy and gratitude, three powerful patterns emerged:

- Without exception, every person I interviewed who described living a joyful life or who described themselves as joyful actively practiced gratitude and attributed their joyfulness to their gratitude practice.
- Both joy and gratitude were described as spiritual practices that were bound to a belief in human interconnectedness and a power greater than us.
- People were quick to point out the difference between happiness and joy as the difference between a human emotion that's connected to circumstances and a spiritual way of engaging with the world that's connected to practicing gratitude.

GRATITUDE

When it comes to gratitude, the word that jumped out at me throughout this research process is *practice*. I don't necessarily think another researcher would have been so taken aback, but as someone who thought that knowledge was more important than practice, I found these words to be a call to action. In fact, it's safe to say that reluctantly recognizing the importance of practice sparked my 2007 ~~Breakdown~~ Spiritual Awakening.

For years, I subscribed to the notion of an "attitude of gratitude." I've since learned that an attitude is an orientation or a way of thinking and that "having an attitude" doesn't always translate to a behavior.

For example, it would be reasonable to say that I have a yoga attitude. The ideals and beliefs that guide my life are very in line with the ideas and beliefs that I associate with yoga. I value mindfulness, breathing, and the body-mind-spirit connection. I even have yoga outfits. But, let me assure you, my yoga attitude and outfits don't mean jack if you put me on a yoga mat and ask me to stand on my head or strike a pose. Why don't they mean jack? I don't *practice* yoga. I don't put my attitude into action enough to call it a practice. So where it really matters—on the mat—my yoga attitude doesn't count for much.

So, what does a gratitude practice look like? The folks I interviewed talked about keeping gratitude journals, doing daily gratitude meditations or prayers, creating gratitude art, and even stopping during their stressful, busy days to actually say these words out loud: "I am grateful for . . ." When the wholehearted talk about gratitude, there are a whole bunch of verbs involved.

It seems that gratitude without practice may be a little like faith without works—it's not alive.

WHAT IS JOY?

Joy seems to me a step beyond happiness. Happiness is a sort of atmosphere you can live in sometimes when you're lucky. Joy is a light that fills you with hope and faith and love.

—ADELA ROGERS ST. JOHNS

The research has taught me that happiness and joy are different experiences. In the interviews, people would often say something like, "Being grateful and joyful doesn't mean that I'm happy all of the time." On many occasions I would delve deeper into those types of statements by asking, "What does it look like when you're joyful and grateful, but not happy?" The answers were all similar: Happiness is tied to circumstance and joyfulness is tied to spirit and gratitude.

I also learned that neither joy nor happiness is constant; no one feels happy all of the time or joyful all of the time. Both experiences come and go. Happiness is attached to external situations and events and seems to ebb and flow as those circumstances come and go. Joy seems to be constantly tethered to our hearts by spirit and gratitude. But our actual experiences of joy—these intense feelings of deep spiritual connection and pleasure—seize us in a very vulnerable way.

After these differences emerged from my data, I looked around to find what other researchers had written about joy and happiness. Interestingly, the explanation that seemed to best describe my findings was from a theologian.

Anne Robertson, a Methodist pastor, writer, and executive director of the Massachusetts Bible Society, explains how the Greek origins of the words *happiness* and *joy* hold important meaning for us today. She explains that the Greek word for happiness is *makarios,* which was used to describe the freedom of the rich from normal cares and worries, or to describe a person who received some form of good fortune, such as money or health. Robertson compares this to the Greek word for joy, which is *chairo.* Chairo was described by the ancient Greeks as the "culmination of being" and the "good mood of the soul." Robertson writes, "Chairo is something, the ancient Greeks tell us, that is found only in God and comes with virtue and wisdom. It isn't a beginner's virtue; it comes as the culmination. They say its opposite is not sadness, but fear."[1]

We need both happiness and joy. I think it's important to create and recognize the experiences that make us happy. In fact, I'm a big fan of Gretchen Rubin's book *The Happiness Project* and Tal Ben-Shahar's research and book *Happier.* But in addition to creating happiness in our lives, I've learned that we need to cultivate the spiritual practices that lead to joyfulness, especially gratitude. In my own life, I'd like to experience more happiness, but I want to *live* from a place of gratitude and joy. To do this, I think we have to take a hard look at the things that get in the way of gratitude and joy, and to some degree, even happiness.

SCARCITY AND FEAR OF THE DARK

The very first time I tried to write about what gets in the way of gratitude and joy, I was sitting on the couch in my living room with my laptop next to me and my research memo journal in my hands. I was tired and rather than writing, I spent an hour staring at the twinkle lights hanging over the entryway into my dining room. I'm a huge fan of those little clear, sparkly lights. I think they make the world look prettier, so I keep them in my house year-round.

As I sat there flipping through the stories and gazing at the twinkle lights, I took out a pen and wrote this down:

> Twinkle lights are the perfect metaphor for joy. Joy is not a constant. It comes to us in moments—often ordinary moments. Sometimes we miss out on the bursts of joy because we're too busy chasing down extraordinary moments. Other times we're so afraid of the dark that we don't dare let ourselves enjoy the light.

> A joyful life is not a floodlight of joy. That would eventually become unbearable.

> I believe a joyful life is made up of joyful moments gracefully strung together by trust, gratitude, inspiration, and faith.

Joy and gratitude can be very vulnerable and intense experiences. We are an anxious people and many of us have very little tolerance for vulnerability. Our anxiety and fear can manifest as scarcity. We think to ourselves:

- I'm not going to allow myself to feel this joy because I know it won't last.

- Acknowledging how grateful I am is an invitation for disaster.
- I'd rather not be joyful than have to wait for the other shoe to drop.

FEAR OF THE DARK

I've always been prone to worry and anxiety, but after I became a mother, negotiating joy, gratitude, and scarcity felt like a full-time job. For years, my fear of something terrible happening to my children actually prevented me from fully embracing joy and gratitude. Every time I came too close to softening into sheer joyfulness about my children and how much I love them, I'd picture something terrible happening; I'd picture losing everything in a flash.

At first I thought I was crazy. Was I the only person in the world who did this? As my therapist and I started working on it, I realized that "my too good to be true" was totally related to fear, scarcity, and vulnerability. Knowing that those are pretty universal emotions, I gathered up the courage to talk about my experiences with a group of five hundred parents who had come to one of my parenting lectures. I gave an example of standing over my daughter watching her sleep, feeling totally engulfed in gratitude, then being ripped out of that joy and gratitude by images of something bad happening to her.

You could have heard a pin drop. I thought, *Oh, God. I'm crazy and now they're all sitting there like, "She's a nut. How do we get out of here?"* Then all of a sudden I heard the sound of a woman toward the back starting to cry. Not sniffle cry, but sob cry. That sound was followed by someone from the front shouting out, "Oh my God! Why do we do that? What does it mean?" The auditorium erupted in some kind of crazy parent revival. As I had suspected, I was not alone. What I didn't know at the time is that I would continue to study what I now call "foreboding joy" for the next decade, and this would lead me to discovering that the best way to transform our compulsive need to dress-rehearse tragedy in times of overwhelming joy is to practice gratitude. Rather than using that vulnerability shiver that comes when things feel "too good" as a warning sign, use it as a reminder to practice gratitude.

Also, know that if joy scares you—you're not alone. Most of us have experienced being on the edge of joy only to be overcome by vulnerability and thrown into fear. Until we can tolerate vulnerability and transform it into gratitude, intense feelings of love will often bring up the fear of loss. If I had to sum up what I've learned about fear and joy, this is what I would say:

> The dark does not destroy the light; it defines it. It's our *fear* of the dark that casts our joy into the shadows.

SCARCITY

These are anxious and fearful times, both of which breed scarcity. We're afraid to lose what we love the most, and we hate that there are no guarantees. We think not being grateful and not feeling joy will make it hurt less. We think if we can beat vulnerability to the punch by imaging loss, we'll suffer less. We're wrong. There is one guarantee: If we're not practicing gratitude and allowing ourselves to know joy, we are missing out on the two things that will actually sustain us during the inevitable hard times.

What I'm describing above is scarcity of safety and uncertainty. But there are other kinds of scarcity. My friend Lynne Twist has written an incredible book called *The Soul of Money*. In this book, Lynne addresses the myth of scarcity. She writes,

> For me, and for many of us, our first waking thought of the day is "I didn't get enough sleep." The next one is "I don't have enough time." Whether true or not, that thought of *not enough* occurs to us automatically before we even think to question or examine it. We spend most of the hours and the days of our lives hearing, explaining, complaining, or worrying about what we don't have enough of. . . . We don't have enough exercise. We don't have enough work. We don't have enough profits. We don't have enough power. We don't have enough wilderness. We don't have enough weekends. Of course, we don't have enough money—ever.
>
> We're not thin enough, we're not smart enough, we're not pretty enough or fit enough or educated or successful enough, or rich enough—ever. Before we even sit up in bed, before our feet touch the floor, we're already inadequate, already behind, already losing, already lacking something. And by the time we go to bed at night, our minds race with a litany of what we didn't get, or didn't get done, that day. We go to sleep bur-

dened by those thoughts and wake up to the reverie of
lack. . . . What begins as a simple expression of the
hurried life, or even the challenged life, grows into the
great justification for an unfulfilled life.[2]

As I read this passage, it makes total sense to me why
we're a nation hungry for more joy: Because we're starving
from a lack of gratitude. Lynne says that addressing scarcity
doesn't mean searching for abundance but rather choosing a
mind-set of sufficiency:

We each have the choice in any setting to step back
and let go of the mind-set of scarcity. Once we let go of
scarcity, we discover the surprising truth of sufficiency.
By sufficiency, I don't mean a quantity of anything.
Sufficiency isn't two steps up from poverty or one step
short of abundance. It isn't a measure of barely enough
or more than enough. Sufficiency isn't an amount at
all. It is an experience, a context we generate, a decla-
ration, a knowing that there is enough, and that we are
enough.
     Sufficiency resides inside of each of us, and we can
call it forward. It is a consciousness, an attention, an
intentional choosing of the way we think about our circumstances.[3]

Scarcity is also great fuel for the gremlins. In my earlier
shame research and in this more recent research, I realized
how many of us have bought into the idea that something has
to be extraordinary if it's going to bring us joy. In *I Thought It*

Was Just Me, I write, "We seem to measure the value of people's contributions (and sometimes their entire lives) by their level of public recognition. In other words, worth is measured by fame and fortune. Our culture is quick to dismiss quiet, ordinary, hardworking people. In many instances, we equate *ordinary* with *boring* or, even more dangerous, *ordinary* has become synonymous with *meaningless.*"[4]

I think I learned the most about the value of ordinary from interviewing people who have experienced tremendous loss such as the loss of a child, violence, genocide, and trauma. The memories that they held most sacred were the ordinary, everyday moments. It was clear that their most precious memories were forged from a collection of ordinary moments, and their hope for others is that they would stop long enough to be grateful for those moments and the joy they bring. Author and spiritual leader Marianne Williamson says, "Joy is what happens to us when we allow ourselves to recognize how good things really are."

DIG DEEP

Get Deliberate: When I'm flooded with fear and scarcity, I try to call forward joy and sufficiency by acknowledging the fear, then transforming it into gratitude. I say this out loud: "I'm feeling vulnerable. That's okay. I'm so grateful for _____." Doing this has absolutely increased my capacity for joy.

Get Inspired: I'm so inspired by the daily doses of joy that happen in those ordinary moments, like walking my kids home from school, jumping on the trampoline, and sharing family meals. Acknowledging that these moments are really what life is about has changed my outlook on work, family, and success.

Get Going: From taking turns being thankful during grace to more creative projects like creating a jar to keep gratitude notes in, we're making wholeheartedness a family affair.

Cultivating Intuition
and Trusting Faith:
Letting Go of the Need
for Certainty

Everything about this research process has pushed me in ways that I never imagined. This is especially true when it comes to topics like faith, intuition, and spirituality. When the importance of intuition and faith first emerged as key patterns in wholehearted living, I winced a little bit. Once again, I felt like my good friends—logic and reason—were under attack. I remember telling Steve, "Now it's intuition and faith! Can you believe it?"

He replied, "I'm surprised that you're surprised. You work off of faith and your gut all of the time."

He took me off guard with his comment.

I sat down next to him and said, "Yeah, I know I'm a gut and faith kinda girl, but I guess I'm not very intuitive. Read this definition from the dictionary: 'Intuition is direct perception of truth or fact, independent of any reasoning process.' "[1]

Steve chuckled. "So, maybe the definition doesn't match what you're learning from the data. You'll write a new one. It won't be the first time."

I spent a year focusing on intuition and faith. I interviewed and collected stories so that I could get my head and heart around what it means to cultivate intuition and trust faith. I was surprised by what I learned.

INTUITION

Intuition is not independent of any reasoning process. In fact, psychologists believe that intuition is a rapid-fire, unconscious associating process—like a mental puzzle.[2] The brain makes an observation, scans its files, and matches the observation with existing memories, knowledge, and experiences. Once it puts together a series of matches, we get a "gut" on what we've observed.

Sometimes our intuition or our gut tells us what we need to know; other times it actually steers us toward fact-finding and reasoning. As it turns out, intuition may be the quiet voice within, but that voice is not limited to one message. Sometimes our intuition whispers, "Follow your instincts." Other times it shouts, "You need to check this out; we don't have enough information!"

In my research, I found that what silences our intuitive voice is our need for certainty. Most of us are not very good at not knowing. We like sure things and guarantees so much that we don't pay attention to the outcomes of our brain's matching process.

For example, rather than respecting a strong internal instinct, we become fearful and look for assurances from others.

- "What do you think?"
- "Should I do it?"
- "Do you think it's a good idea, or do you think I'll regret it?"
- "What would you do?"

A typical response to these survey questions is, "I'm not sure what you should do. What does your gut say?"

And there it is. *What does your gut say?*

We shake our head and say, "I'm not sure" when the real answer is, "I have no idea what my gut says; we haven't spoken in years."

When we start polling people, it's often because we don't trust our own knowing. It feels too shaky and too uncertain. We want assurances and folks with whom we can share the blame if things don't pan out. I know all about this. I'm a professional pollster—it's hard for me to go it alone sometimes. When I'm making a difficult decision and feel disconnected from my intuition, I have a tendency to survey everyone around me. Ironically, since doing this research, surveying has become a red flag for me—it tells me that I'm feeling vulnerable about making a decision.

As I mentioned earlier, if we learn to trust our intuition, it can even tell us that we don't have a good instinct on something and that we need more data. Another example of how our need for certainty sabotages our intuition is when we ignore our gut's warning to slow down, gather more information, or reality-check our expectations:

- "I'm just going to do it. I don't care anymore."
- "I'm tired of thinking about it. It's too stressful."
- "I'd rather just do it than wait another second."
- "I can't stand not knowing."

When we charge headlong into big decisions, it may be because we don't want to know the answers that will emerge from doing due diligence. We know that fact-finding might lead us away from what we think we want.

I always tell myself, "If I'm afraid to run the numbers or put pencil to paper, I shouldn't do it." When we just want to get the decision-making over with, it's a good idea to ask ourselves whether we simply can't stand the vulnerability of being still long enough to think it through and make a mindful decision.

So, as you can see, intuition isn't always about accessing the answers from within. Sometimes when we've tapped into our inner wisdom, it tells us that we don't know enough to make a decision without more investigation. Here's the definition I crafted from the research:

Intuition is not a single way of knowing—it's our ability to hold space for uncertainty and our willingness to trust the many ways we've developed knowledge and insight, including instinct, experience, faith, and reason.

FAITH

I've come to realize that faith and reason are not natural enemies. It's our human need for certainty and our need to "be right" that have pitted faith and reason against each other in an almost reckless way. We force ourselves to choose and defend one way of knowing the world at the expense of the other.

I understand that faith and reason can clash and create uncomfortable tensions—those tensions play out in my life, and I can feel them in my bones. But this work has forced me to see that it's our fear of the unknown and our fear of being wrong that create most of our conflict and anxiety. We need both faith and reason to make meaning in an uncertain world.

I can't tell you how many times I've heard the terms *having faith* and *my faith* in my interviews with people who are living the wholehearted journey. At first I thought that faith meant "there's a reason for everything." I personally struggled with that because I'm not comfortable with using God or faith or spirituality to explain tragedy. It actually feels like substituting certainty for faith when people say, "There's a reason for everything."

But I quickly learned from the interviews that faith meant something else to these people. Here's how I define *faith* based on the research interviews:

Faith is a place of mystery, where we find the courage to believe in what we cannot see and the strength to let go of our fear of uncertainty.

I also learned that it's not always the scientists who struggle with faith and the religious who fully embrace uncertainty. Many forms of fundamentalism and extremism are about choosing certainty over faith.

I love this from theologian Richard Rohr: "My scientist friends have come up with things like 'principles of uncertainty' and dark holes. They're willing to live inside imagined hypotheses and theories. But many religious folks insist on *answers* that are *always* true. We love closure, resolution and clarity, while thinking that we are people of 'faith'! How strange that the very word 'faith' has come to mean its exact opposite."[3]

Faith is essential when we decide to live and love with our whole hearts in a world where most of us want assurances before we risk being vulnerable and getting hurt. To say, "I'm going to engage wholeheartedly in my life" requires believing without seeing.

DIG DEEP

Get Deliberate: Letting go of certainty is one of my greatest challenges. I even have a physical response to "not knowing"— it's anxiety and fear and vulnerability combined. That's when I have to get very quiet and still. With my busy life, that can mean hiding in the garage or driving around the block. Whatever it takes, I have to find a way to be still so I can hear what I'm saying.

Get Inspired: The process of reclaiming my spiritual and faith life was not an easy one (hence the 2007 ~~Breakdown~~

Spiritual Awakening). There's a quote that literally cracked open my heart. It's from a book by Anne Lamott: "The opposite of faith is not doubt, but certainty."[4] Her books about faith and grace inspire me.[5] I'm inspired by and thankful for *When the Heart Waits* by Sue Monk Kidd[6] and Pema Chödrön's *Comfortable with Uncertainty*;[7] they saved me. And last, I absolutely love this quote from Paulo Coelho's *The Alchemist*: ". . . intuition is really a sudden immersion of the soul into the universal current of life, where the histories of all people are connected, and we are able to know everything, because it's all written there."[8]

Get Going: When I'm really scared or unsure, I need something right away to calm my cravings for certainty. For me, the Serenity Prayer does the trick. *God, grant me the serenity to accept the things I cannot change, the courage to change the things I can, and the wisdom to know the difference.* Amen!

Cultivating Creativity: Letting Go of Comparison

Some of my best childhood memories involve creativity, and almost all of them are from the years that we lived in New Orleans, in a funky pink stucco duplex a couple of blocks from Tulane University. I remember my mom and me spending hours painting wooden key chains shaped like turtles and snails, and making crafts out of sequins and felt with my friends.

I can vividly see my mom and her friends in their bell-bottoms coming home from the market in the French Quarter and making stuffed mirlitons and other delicious dishes. I was so fascinated with helping her in the kitchen that one Sunday afternoon she and my dad let me cook alone. They said I could make anything I wanted with any ingredient that I wanted. I made oatmeal-raisin cookies. With crawfish boil spices instead of cinnamon. The entire house stank for days.

My mom also loved to sew. She made matching shift dresses that she and I wore (along with my doll, who also had her own tiny matching dress). It's so strange to me that all of these memories that involve creating are so real and textured to me—I can almost feel them and smell them. They also hold so much tender meaning.

Sadly, my memories of creating end around age eight or nine. In fact, I don't have a single creativity memory after about fifth grade. That was the same time that we moved from our tiny house in the Garden District to a big house in a sprawling Houston suburb. Everything seemed to change. In New Orleans, every wall in our house was covered with art done by my mom or a relative or us kids, and homemade curtains hung over every window. The art and curtains may have been out of necessity, but I remember it being beautiful.

In Houston, I remember walking into some of my new neighbors' houses and thinking that their living rooms looked like the lobby of a fancy hotel—I vividly remember thinking at the time, *like a Howard Johnson or a Holiday Inn.* There were long heavy drapes, big sofas with matching chairs, and shiny glass tables. There were plastic plants with hanging vines strategically sitting on top of armoires, and dried flowers in baskets decorating the tops of tables. Strangely, everyone's lobby kinda looked the same.

While the houses were all the same and fancy, the school was a different story. In New Orleans, I went to a Catholic school and everyone looked the same, prayed the same, and, for the most part, acted the same. In Houston I started public school, which meant no more uniforms. In this new school, cute clothes counted. And not homemade cute clothes, but clothes from "the mall."

In New Orleans, my dad worked during the day and was a law student at Loyola at night. There was always an informal and fun feel to our lives there. Once we got to Houston, he dressed up every morning and commuted to an oil and gas corporation along with every other father in our neighborhood. Things changed, and in many ways that move felt like a fundamental shift for our family. My parents were launched on the accomplishments-and-acquisitions track, and creativity gave way to that stifling combination of fitting in and being better than, also known as comparison.

Comparison is all about conformity and competition. At first it seems like conforming and competing are mutually exclusive, but they're not. When we compare, we want to see who or what is best out of a specific collection of "alike things." We may compare things like how we parent with parents who have totally different values or traditions than us, but the comparisons that get us really riled up are the ones we make with the folks living next door, or on our child's soccer team, or at our school. We don't compare our houses to the mansions across town; we compare our yard to the yards on our block. When we compare, we want to be the best or have the best of our group.

The comparison mandate becomes this crushing paradox of "fit in and stand out!" It's not "cultivate self-acceptance, belonging, and authenticity"; it's "be just like everyone else, but better."

It's easy to see how difficult it is to make time for the important things such as creativity, gratitude, joy, and authenticity when we're spending enormous amounts of energy conforming and competing. Now I understand the quote from Theodore Roosevelt: "Comparison is the thief of joy." I can't tell you how many times I'm feeling so good about myself and my life and my family, and then in a split second it's gone because I consciously or unconsciously start comparing myself to other people.

As far as my own story, the older I got, the less value I put on creativity and the less time I spent creating. When people asked me about crafting or art or creating, I relied on the standard, "I'm not the creative type." On the inside I was really thinking, *Who has time for painting and scrapbooking and photography when the real work of achieving and accomplishing needs to be done?*

By the time I was forty and working on this research, my lack of interest in creativity had turned into disdain. I'm not sure if I would categorize my feelings about creativity as negative stereotypes, shame triggers, or some combination of the two, but it came to the point where I thought of creating for the sake of creating as self-indulgent at best and flaky at worst.

Of course I know, professionally, that the more entrenched and reactive we are about an issue, the more we need to investigate our responses. As I look back with new eyes, I think tapping into how much I missed that part of my life would have been too confusing or painful.

I never thought I'd come across something fierce enough to shake me loose from my entrenched beliefs about creativity. Then this research came along . . .

Let me sum up what I've learned about creativity from the world of wholehearted living and loving:

1. "I'm not very creative" doesn't work. There's no such thing as creative people and non-creative

people. There are only people who use their creativity and people who don't. Unused creativity
doesn't just disappear. It lives within us until it's
expressed, neglected to death, or suffocated by resentment and fear.

2. The only unique contribution that we will ever
    make in this world will be born of our creativity.

3. If we want to make meaning, we need to make
    art. Cook, write, draw, doodle, paint, scrapbook,
    take pictures, collage, knit, rebuild an engine,
    sculpt, dance, decorate, act, sing—it doesn't mat-
    ter. As long as we're creating, we're cultivating
    meaning.

Literally one month after I worked through the data on
creativity, I signed up for a gourd-painting class at Casa
Ramirez in Houston. I'm not even kidding. I went with my
mom and Ellen, and it was one of the best days of my life.

For the first time in decades, I started creating. And I
haven't stopped. I even took up photography. It might sound
cliché, but the world doesn't even look the same to me anymore. I see beauty and potential everywhere—in my front
yard, at a junk store, in an old magazine—everywhere.

It's been a very emotional transition for me and for my
family. Both of my kids love art, and we do family projects
together all the time. Steve and I are Mac addicts, and we love
to make movies together. Ellen grew up saying she wanted to
be a chef or a "life artist" like my friend Ali Edwards, who in-

spires both of us. Charlie loves to write and plays the guitar. There is nothing better than a house filled with art and music—*homemade* art and music.

I also realized that much of what I do in my work is creative work. Writer William Plomer described creativity as "the power to connect the seemingly unconnected." My work is all about making connections, so part of my transformation was owning and celebrating my existing creativity.

Letting go of comparison is not a to-do list item. For most of us, it's something that requires constant awareness. It's so easy to take our eyes off our path to check out what others are doing and if they're ahead or behind us. Creativity, which is the expression of our originality, helps us stay mindful that what we bring to the world is completely original and cannot be compared. And, without comparison, concepts like *ahead* or *behind* or *best* or *worst* lose their meaning.

DIG DEEP

Get Deliberate: If creativity is seen as a luxury or something we do when we have spare time, it will never be cultivated. I carve out time every week to take and process photographs, make movies, and do art projects with the kids. When I make creating a priority, everything in my life works better.

Get Inspired: Nothing inspires me more than my friendships with the artists, writers, designers, and photographers in my life—many of whom I met online. I think it's so important to find and be a part of a community of like-spirited people who share your beliefs about creativity. There's nothing like geeking out about fonts for an hour over coffee with a friend.

Get Going: Take a class. Risk feeling vulnerable and new and imperfect and take a class. There are wonderful online classes if you need more flexibility. Try something that scares you or something you've dreamt about trying. You never know where you'll find your creative inspiration.

Cultivating Play and Rest: Letting Go of Exhaustion as a Status Symbol and Productivity as Self-Worth

At times, when I was interviewing people for my research, I felt like an alien—like a visitor trying to figure out the customs and habits of people living lives that looked incredibly different from mine. There were many awkward moments when I struggled to understand what *they, the wholehearted,* were doing and why. Sometimes the concepts were so foreign to me that I didn't have the language to name them. This was one of those times.

I remember telling one of my colleagues, "These wholehearted people fool around a lot." She laughed and asked, "Fool around? How?"

I shrugged. "I don't know. They have fun and . . . I don't know what you call it. They hang out and do fun things."

She looked confused. "Like what kind of fun things? Hobbies? Crafts? Sports?"

"Yes," I replied. "Kinda like that but not so organized. I'm going to have to dig around some more."

Now I look back on that conversation and think, *How did I not know what I was seeing?* Was I so personally removed from this concept that I couldn't recognize it?

It's *play*! A critically important component of whole-hearted living is play!

I came to this realization by watching my children and recognizing the same playful behaviors in them that were described by the people I interviewed. These folks play.

Researching the concept of play got off to a rocky start. I learned this very quickly: Do *not* Google "Adult play." I was closing pornography pop-ups so fast it was like playing Whac-A-Mole.

Once I recovered from that search disaster, I was lucky enough to find the work of Dr. Stuart Brown. Dr. Brown is a psychiatrist, clinical researcher, and founder of the National Institute for Play. He is also the author of a wonderful book titled, *Play: How It Shapes the Brain, Opens the Imagination, and Invigorates the Soul.*[1]

Drawing on his own research, as well as the latest advances in biology, psychology, and neurology, Brown explains that play shapes our brain, helps us foster empathy, helps us navigate complex social groups, and is at the core of creativity and innovation.

If you're wondering why play and rest are paired together in this guidepost, it's because after reading the research on play, I now understand that play is as essential to our health and functioning as rest.

So, if you're like me, you want to know, "What exactly is

play?" Brown proposes seven properties of play, the first of which is that play is apparently purposeless. Basically this means that we play for the sake of play. We do it because it's fun and we want to.

Well, this is where my work as a shame researcher comes in. In today's culture—where our self-worth is tied to our net worth, and we base our worthiness on our level of productivity—spending time doing purposeless activities is rare. In fact, for many of us it sounds like an anxiety attack waiting to happen.

We've got so much to do and so little time that the idea of spending time doing anything unrelated to the to-do list actually creates stress. We convince ourselves that playing is a waste of precious time. We even convince ourselves that sleep is a terrible use of our time.

We've got to *get 'er done!* It doesn't matter if our job is running a multimillion-dollar company, raising a family, creating art, or finishing school, we've got to keep our noses to the grindstone and work! There's no time to play around!

But Brown argues that play is not an option. In fact he writes, "The opposite of play is not work—the opposite of play is depression." He explains, "Respecting our biologically programmed need for play can transform work. It can bring back excitement and newness to our job. Play helps us deal with difficulties, provides a sense of expansiveness, promotes mastery of our craft, and is an essential part of the creative process. Most important, true play that comes from our own inner needs and desires is the only path to finding lasting joy and satisfaction in our work. In the long run, work does not work without play."[2]

What's shocking is the similarity between the biological need for play and our body's need for rest, a topic that also emerged as a major theme in wholehearted living. It seems that living and loving with our whole hearts requires us to respect our bodies' need for renewal. When I first researched the ideas of rest, sleep, and *sleep debt*—the term for not getting enough—I couldn't believe some of the consequences of not getting proper rest.

According to the Centers for Disease Control, insufficient sleep is associated with a number of chronic diseases and conditions, such as diabetes, heart disease, obesity, and depression.[3] We're also learning that drowsy driving can be as dangerous—and as preventable—as driving while intoxicated. Yet, somehow many of us still believe that exhaustion is a status symbol of hard work and that sleep is a luxury. The result is that we are so very tired. Dangerously tired.

The same gremlins that tell us we're too busy to play and waste time fooling around are the ones that whisper:

- "One more hour of work! You can catch up on your sleep this weekend."
- "Napping is for the weak."
- "Push through. You can handle it."

But the truth is, we can't handle it. We are a nation of exhausted and overstressed adults raising overscheduled children. We use our spare time to desperately search for joy and meaning in our lives. We think accomplishments and acquisitions will bring joy and meaning, but that pursuit could be the very thing that's keeping us so tired and afraid to slow down.

If we want to live a wholehearted life, we have to become intentional about cultivating sleep and play, and about letting go of exhaustion as a status symbol and productivity as self-worth.

Making the choice to rest and play is, at best, counterculture. The decision to let go of exhaustion and productivity as badges of honor made total sense to Steve and me, but putting wholeheartedness into practice has been a struggle for our entire family.

Steve and I sat down in 2008 and made a practical list of the things that make our family work. We basically answered the question, "When things are going really well in our family, what does it look like?" The answers included sleep, working out, healthy food, cooking, time off, weekends away, going to church, being present with the kids, a sense of control over our money, meaningful work that doesn't consume us, time to piddle, time with family and close friends, alone time, and time to just hang out. These were (and are) our "ingredients for joy and meaning."

Then we looked at the dream list that we started making a couple of years earlier (and kept adding to). Everything on this list was an accomplishment or an acquisition—a house with more bedrooms, a trip here, personal salary goals, professional endeavors, and so forth. Everything required that we make more money and spend more money.

When we compared our dream list to our "joy and meaning" list, we realized that by merely letting go of the list of things we want to accomplish and acquire, we would be actually living our dream—not striving to make it happen in the future, but living it right now. The things we were working toward did nothing in terms of making our life fuller.

Embracing our "joy and meaning" list has not been easy. There are days when it makes perfect sense, and then there are days when I get sucked into believing how much better everything would feel if we just had a really great guest room or a better kitchen, or if I got to speak here or write an article for that popular magazine.

Even our kids had to make some changes. We limit extracurricular activities and help our kids choose what's the most meaningful when it comes to sports, extracurriculars, and other activities. Sometimes they push back because they feel like they're not signed up for as many things as their friends, but when we walk through our family joy and meaning list, they get it. We also insist that their school goals include as many dances as AP courses. And sleep is *not* something we negotiate in our house.

While this approach made and still makes sense for our family, there were times when it was terrifying for me as a parent. What if I'm wrong? What if busy and exhausted is what it takes? What if they don't get to go to the college of their choice because they don't play the violin and don't speak Mandarin and French and don't play six sports?

What if we're normal and quiet and happy? Does that count?

I guess the answer to this is only *yes* if it counts to us. If what matters to us is what we're concerned about, then play and rest is important. If what matters to us is what other people think or say or value, then it's back to exhaustion and producing for self-worth.

Today, I choose play and rest.

DIG DEEP

Get Deliberate: One of the best things that we've ever done in our family is making the "ingredients for joy and meaning" list. I encourage you to sit down and make a list of the specific conditions that are in place when everything feels good in your life. Then check that list against your to-do list and your to-accomplish list. It might surprise you.

Get Inspired: I'm continually inspired by Stuart Brown's work on play and Daniel Pink's book *A Whole New Mind*.[4] If you want to learn more about the importance of play and rest, read these books.

Get Going: Say *no* today. Buck the system. Take something off your list and add "take a nap."

Cultivating Calm and Stillness: Letting Go of Anxiety as a Lifestyle

After this research first emerged, remember that I made a beeline for my therapist's office. I knew my life was out of balance, and I wanted more of what I was learning about in my study. I also wanted to figure out why I was having dizzy spells whenever I got really anxious and stressed out. I would actually get lightheaded, and the room would start to spin. A couple of times, I literally fell over.

The dizziness was new; the anxiety was not. Before I started learning about wholehearted living, I had always been able to manage the competing priorities, the family demands, and the unrelenting pressure of academic life. In many ways, anxiety was a constant in my life.

But as I started developing an awareness about wholehearted living, it's as if my body said, "I'm going to help you embrace this new way of living by making it very difficult for you to ignore anxiety." If I became too anxiety ridden, I'd literally have to sit down or risk falling.

I remember telling Diana, my therapist, "I can't function this way any longer. I really can't."

She replied, "I know. I see that. What do you think you need?"

I thought about it for a second and said, "I need a way to stay on my feet when I'm really anxious."

She just sat there nodding her head and waiting, like therapists do. Waiting and waiting and waiting.

Finally, it dawned on me. "Oh. I get it. I can't function *this way*. I can't function in this much anxiety anymore. I don't need to figure out a way to keep going with this level of anxiety—I need to figure out how to be less anxious."

That silence thing can be effective. It's a pain in the ass, but nonetheless effective.

I used my research to formulate a plan to lessen my anxiety. The people I interviewed weren't anxiety-free or even anxiety-averse; they were anxiety-aware. They were committed to a way of living where anxiety was a reality but not a lifestyle. They did this by cultivating calm and stillness in their lives and making these practices the norm.

Calm and stillness may sound like the same things, but I learned that they are different and that we need both.

CALM

I define *calm* as *creating perspective and mindfulness while managing emotional reactivity*. When I think about calm people, I think about people who can bring perspective to complicated situations and feel their feelings without reacting to heightened emotions like fear and anger.

When I was pregnant with Ellen, someone gave me a small book called *Baby Love: A Tradition of Calm Parenting* by Maud Bryt.[1] Bryt's mother, grandmother, and great-grandmother were midwives in Holland and the book draws on their wisdom. I can still see myself sitting in my brand-new glider with one hand resting on my very pregnant belly and the other hand holding that book. I remember thinking, *This is my goal. I want to be a calm parent.*

Surprisingly, I am a pretty calm parent. Not because it comes naturally to me, but because I practice. A lot. I also have an incredible role model in my husband, Steve. By watching him, I've learned about the value of bringing perspective and quiet to difficult situations.

I try to be slow to respond and quick to think, *Do we even have all the information we need to make a decision or form a response?* I also stay very mindful about the effect that calm has on an anxious person or situation. A panicked response produces more panic and more fear. As psychologist and writer Harriet Lerner says, "Anxiety is extremely contagious, but so is calm."[2] The question becomes, *Do we want to infect people with more anxiety, or heal ourselves and the people around us with calm?*

If we choose to heal with calm, we have to commit to practicing calm. Small things matter. For example, before we respond we can count to ten or give ourselves permission to say, "I'm not sure. I need to think about this some more." It's also extremely effective to identify the emotions that are the most likely to spark your reactivity and then practice non-reactive responses.

A while back there was this powerful public service announcement that showed a couple screaming at each other and slamming the door in each other's faces. They were shouting things like, "I hate you!" and "Mind your own business!" and "I don't want to talk to you." As you watched it, you had no idea why they kept saying these things, slamming the door, and then starting over. After about twenty seconds of the slamming and yelling, the couple held hands and walked away from the door. One of them says to the other, "I think we're ready." The commercial then cut to the announcer, who said something like, "Talk to your kids about drugs. It's not easy, but it could save their lives."

The commercial is a great example of practicing calm. Unless we had calm modeled by our parents and grew up practicing it, it's unlikely that it will be our default response to anxious or emotionally volatile situations.

For me, breathing is the best place to start. Just taking a breath before I respond slows me down and immediately starts spreading calm. Sometimes I actually think to myself, *I'm dying to freak out here! Do I have enough information to freak out? Will freaking out help?* The answer is always *no.*

STILLNESS

The concept of stillness is less complicated than the concept of calm but, for me at least, way more difficult to put into practice.

I wish I could tell you how much I resisted even hearing people describe stillness as an integral part of their wholehearted journey. From meditation and prayer to regular periods of quiet reflection and alone time, the research participants spoke about the necessity of quieting their bodies and minds as a way to feel less anxious and overwhelmed.

I'm sure my resistance to this idea comes from the fact that just thinking about meditating makes me anxious. When I try to meditate, I feel like a total poser. I spend the entire time thinking about how I need to stop thinking, *Okay, I'm not thinking about anything. I'm not thinking about anything. Milk, laundry detergent . . . stop! Okay, not thinking. Not thinking. Oh, man. Is this over yet?*

I don't want to admit it, but the truth is that stillness used to be very anxiety provoking for me. In my mind, being still was narrowly defined as sitting cross-legged on the floor and focusing on that elusive nothingness. As I collected and analyzed more stories, I realized that my initial thinking was wrong. Here's the definition of *stillness* that emerged from the data:

> Stillness is not about focusing on nothingness; it's about creating a clearing. It's opening up an emotionally clutter-free space and allowing ourselves to feel and think and dream and question.

Once we can let go of our assumptions about what stillness is supposed to look like and find a way to create a clearing that works for us, we stand a better chance of opening ourselves up and confronting the next barrier to stillness: fear. And it can be big, big fear.

If we stop long enough to create a quiet emotional clearing, the truth of our lives will invariably catch up with us. We convince ourselves that if we stay busy enough and keep moving, reality won't be able to keep up. So we stay in front of the truth about how tired and scared and confused and overwhelmed we sometimes feel. Of course, the irony is that the thing that's wearing us down is trying to stay out in front of feeling worn down. This is the self-perpetuating quality of anxiety. It feeds on itself. I often say that when they start having Twelve Step meetings for busy-aholics, they'll need to rent out football stadiums.

In addition to fear, another barrier that gets in the way of both stillness and calm is how we're raised to think about these practices. From very early in our lives, we get confusing messages about the value of calm and stillness. Parents and teachers scream, "Calm down!" and "Sit still!" rather than actually modeling the behaviors they want to see. So instead of becoming practices that we want to cultivate, calm gives way to perpetuating anxiety, and the idea of stillness makes us feel jumpy.

In our increasingly complicated and anxious world, we need more time to do less and be less. When we first start cultivating calm and stillness in our lives, it can be difficult, especially when we realize how stress and anxiety define so much of our daily lives. But as our practices become stronger, anxiety loses its hold and we gain clarity about what we're doing, where we're going, and what holds true meaning for us.

DIG DEEP

Get Deliberate: My anxiety detox included more calm and more stillness, but it also included more exercise and less caffeine. I know so many people who take something at night to help them sleep and drink caffeine all day to stay awake. Calm and stillness are potent medicine for general sleeplessness and a lack of energy. Increasing my daily intake of calm and stillness along with walking and swimming and cutting caffeine has done wonders for my life.

Get Inspired: I remain inspired and transformed by something I learned from Harriet Lerner's book *The Dance of Connection*.[3] Dr. Lerner explains that we all have patterned ways of managing anxiety. Some of us respond to anxiety by *over*functioning and others by *under*functioning. Overfunctioners tend to move quickly to advise, rescue, take over, micromanage, and get in other people's business rather than look inward. Underfunctioners tend to get less competent under stress. They invite others to take over and often become the focus of family gossip, worry, or concern. They can get labeled as the "irresponsible one" or the "problem child" or the "fragile one." Dr. Lerner explains that seeing these behaviors as patterned responses to anxiety, rather than truths about who we are, can help us understand that we can change. Overfunctioners, like me, can become more willing to embrace our vulnerabilities in the face of anxiety, and underfunctioners can work to amplify their strengths and competencies.

Get Going: Experiment with different forms of still and quiet. We all need to find something that works for us. To be honest, I'm never more open and emotionally clutter-free than when I'm walking alone outside. It's not technically still, but it's an emotional opening for me.

Cultivating Meaningful Work: Letting Go of Self-Doubt and "Supposed To"

In the chapter on creativity, I wrote that a significant part of my work involves making connections. In fact, the heart of my work is finding and naming the subtle and often unspoken connections between how we think, feel, and act. Sometimes the connections are easy to spot and fall right into place. Other times they are elusive, and trying to put things together feels messy and tangled. This guidepost started out as one of those messy and tangled experiences, but with time, I learned about some striking connections.

Early in this research, it was clear to me that living a wholehearted life included engaging in what many people I interviewed called *meaningful work*. Others spoke of having a calling. And some simply described feeling a tremendous sense of accomplishment and purpose from their work. It all seemed pretty straightforward, except for this pesky list of words that emerged as being important and somehow *connected* to the quest for meaningful work:

- gifts and talents
- spirituality
- making a living
- commitment
- supposed to's
- self-doubt

I say pesky because it took me a long time to figure out how they all worked together. The exhausted part of me wanted to forget about these "extra" words, much like what Steve does when he puts together furniture from IKEA and there are twelve unused screws when he's done. I wanted to stand back, give it a little shake, and say, "Good enough! These must be extras."

But I couldn't. So I took apart the idea of meaningful work, interviewed more participants, found the connections, and rebuilt the guidepost. This is what emerged:

- *We all have gifts and talents.* When we cultivate those gifts and share them with the world, we create a sense of meaning and purpose in our lives.
- *Squandering our gifts brings distress to our lives.* As it turns out, it's not merely benign or "too bad" if we don't use the gifts that we've been given; we pay for it with our emotional and physical well-being. When we don't use our talents to cultivate meaningful work, we struggle. We feel disconnected and

weighed down by feelings of emptiness, frustration, resentment, shame, disappointment, fear, and even grief.

- Most of us who are searching for spiritual connection spend too much time looking up at the sky and wondering why God lives so far away. God lives within us, not above us. *Sharing our gifts and talents with the world is the most powerful source of connection with God.*

- *Using our gifts and talents to create meaningful work takes a tremendous amount of commitment,* because in many cases the meaningful work is not what pays the bills. Some folks have managed to align everything—they use their gifts and talents to do work that feeds their souls and their families; however, most people piece it together.

- No one can define what's meaningful for us. Culture doesn't get to dictate if it's working outside the home, raising children, lawyering, teaching, or painting. *Like our gifts and talents, meaning is unique to each one of us.*

SELF-DOUBT AND "SUPPOSED TO"

The gauntlet of gremlins can get in the way of cultivating meaningful work. They start by taunting us about our gifts and talents:

- "Maybe everyone has special gifts . . . *except for you.* Maybe that's why you haven't found them yet."

- "Yes, you do that well, but that's not really a gift.
  It's not big enough or important enough to be a real
  talent."

Self-doubt undermines the process of finding our gifts and sharing them with the world. Moreover, if developing and sharing our gifts is how we honor spirit and connect with God, self-doubt is letting our fear undermine our faith.

The gremlins get lots of mileage out of "supposed to"—the battle cry of fitting in, perfectionism, people-pleasing, and proving ourselves:

- "You're supposed to care about making money, not
  meaning."
- "You're supposed to grow up and be a
  _____. Everyone's counting on it."
- "You're supposed to hate your work; that's the
  definition of work."
- "If you're brave, you're supposed to quit your job and
  follow your bliss. Don't worry about money!"
- "You're supposed to choose: Work you love or work
  that supports the people you love."

To overcome self-doubt and "supposed to," we have to start owning the messages. What makes us afraid? What's on our "supposed to" list? Who says? Why?

Gremlins are like toddlers. If you ignore them, they get louder. It's usually best to just acknowledge the messages. Write them down. I know it seems counterintuitive, but writing them down and owning the gremlins' messages doesn't give the messages more power; it gives us more power. It gives us the opportunity to say, "I get it. I see that I'm afraid of this, but I'm going to do it anyway."

NICE TO MEET YOU. WHAT DO YOU DO?

In addition to the gremlins, another thing that gets in the way of meaningful work is the struggle to define who we are and what we do in an honest way. In a world that values the primacy of work, the most common question that we ask and get asked is, "What do you do?" I used to wince every time someone asked me this question. I felt like my choices were to reduce myself to an easily digestible sound bite or to confuse the hell out of people.

Now my answer to "What do you do?" is, "How much time do you have?"

Most of us have complicated answers to this question. For example, I'm a mom, partner, researcher, writer, storyteller, sister, friend, daughter, and teacher. All of these things make up who I am, so I never know how to answer that question. And, to be honest with you, I'm tired of choosing to make it easier on the person who asked.

In 2009, I met Marci Alboher, an author/speaker/coach. If you're wondering what's up with the slashes, I think they're very appropriate as Marci is the author of *One Person/Multiple Careers: A New Model for Work/Life Success.*[1]

Alboher interviewed hundreds of people pursuing multiple careers simultaneously and discovered how slash careers—researcher/storyteller, artist/real estate agent—integrate and fully express the multiple passions, talents, and interests that a single career cannot accommodate. Marci's book is full of stories about people who have created meaningful work by refusing to be defined by a single career. Examples include a longshoreman/documentary filmmaker, a management consultant/cartoonist, a lawyer/chef, a rabbi/stand-up comic, a surgeon/playwright, an investment manager/rapper, and a therapist/violin maker.

I wanted to share the idea of the slash effect with you because in the art and writing world, I meet so many people who are afraid to claim their work. For example, I recently met a woman at a social media conference who is an accountant/jeweler. I was excited to meet her, because I had bought a beautiful pair of earrings from her online. When I asked her how long she had been a jeweler, she blushed and said, "I wish. I'm a CPA. I'm not a real jeweler."

I thought to myself, *I'm wearing your earrings right now, not your abacus.* When I pointed to my ears and said, "Of course you're a jewelry maker!" she just smiled and replied, "I don't make very much money doing that. I just do it because I love it." As ludicrous as that sounded to me, I get it. I hate calling myself a writer because it doesn't feel legitimate to me. I'm not writer *enough.* Overcoming self-doubt is all about believing we're enough and letting go of what the world says we're supposed to be and supposed to call ourselves.

Every semester I share this quote by theologian Howard Thurman with my graduate students. It's always been one of my favorites, but now that I've studied the importance of meaningful work, it's taken on new significance: "Don't ask what the world needs. Ask what makes you come alive, and go do it. Because what the world needs is people who have come alive."

DIG DEEP

Get Deliberate: It can take some time to figure out how to get deliberate about doing meaningful work. I finally got very specific and wrote down my own criteria for "meaningful." Right now, just for me, I want my work to be inspiring, contemplative, and creative. I'm using these as a filter to make decisions about what I do/what I commit to/how I spend my time.

Get Inspired: I highly recommend Marci Alboher's *One Person/Multiple Careers*. It includes lots of practical strategies for living the slash. Malcom Gladwell is also a constant source of inspiration for me. In his book *Outliers,* Gladwell proposes that there are three criteria for meaningful work—complexity, autonomy, and a relationship between effort and reward—and that these can often be found in creative work.[2] These criteria absolutely fit with what cultivating meaningful work means in the context of the wholehearted journey. Last, I think everyone should read Paulo Coelho's *The Alchemist*[3]— I try to read it at least once a year. It's a powerful way of seeing the connections between our gifts, our spirituality, and our work (slashed or not) and how they come together to create meaning in our lives.

Get Going: Make a list of the work that inspires you. Don't be practical. Don't think about making a living; think about doing something you love. There's nothing that says you have to quit your day job to cultivate meaningful work. There's also nothing that says your day job isn't meaningful work—maybe you've just never thought of it that way. What's your ideal slash? What do you want to be when you grow up? What brings meaning to you?

Cultivating Laughter, Song, and Dance: Letting Go of Being Cool and "Always in Control"

Throughout human history, we've relied on laughter, song, and dance to express ourselves, to communicate our stories and emotions, to celebrate and mourn, and to nurture community. While most people would tell you that a life without laughter, music, and dance would be unbearable, it's easy to take these experiences for granted.

Laughter, song, and dance are so woven into the fabric of our everyday life that we can forget how much we value the people who can make us laugh, the songs that inspire us to roll down the car window and sing at the top of our lungs, and the total freedom we feel when we throw an impromptu family dance party in the kitchen.

In her book *Dancing in the Streets: A History of Collective Joy,* social critic Barbara Ehrenreich draws on history and anthropology to document the importance of engaging in what she refers to as "collective ecstasy." Ehrenreich concludes that we are "innately social beings, impelled almost instinctively to share our joy."[1] I absolutely believe she is right. I also love the idea of collective ecstasy—especially now, when we seem to be stuck in a state of collective fear and anxiety.

As I sifted through my data, I asked myself two questions:

1. Why are laughter, song, and dance so important to us?

2. Is there some transformational element that they have in common?

These were complicated questions to answer because, yes, we yearn to laugh and sing and dance when we feel joy, but we also turn to these forms of expression when we feel lonely, sad, excited, in love, heartbroken, afraid, ashamed, confident, certain, doubtful, brave, grief, and ecstasy (just to name a few). I'm convinced that there's a song, a dance, and a path to laughter for every human emotion.

After a couple of years of analyzing my data, here's what I learned:

Laughter, song, and dance create emotional and spiritual connection; they remind us of the one thing that truly matters when we are searching for comfort, celebration, inspiration, or healing: We are not alone.

Ironically, I learned the most about laughter during the eight years that I was studying shame. Shame resilience requires laughter. In *I Thought It Was Just Me,* I refer to the kind of laughter that helps us heal as *knowing laughter.* Laughter is a spiritual form of communing; without words we can say to one another, "I'm with you. I get it."

True laughter is not the use of humor as self-deprecation or deflection; it's not the kind of painful laughter we sometimes hide behind. Knowing laughter embodies the relief and connection we experience when we realize the power of sharing our stories—we're not laughing *at* each other but *with* each other.

One of my favorite definitions of laughter comes from writer Anne Lamott, whom I once heard say, "Laughter is a bubbly, effervescent form of holiness." Amen!

SONG

From the eight-track tapes my parents played in our station wagon to my stack of vinyl records from the 1970s to my mixtapes from the '80s and '90s to the playlists on my iPhone, my life has a soundtrack. And the songs from that soundtrack can stir memories and provoke emotion in me like nothing else.

I realize that not everyone shares the same passion for music, but the one thing that is universal about song is its ability to move us emotionally—sometimes in ways we don't even think about. For example, I was recently watching the director's cut of a movie. It showed a very dramatic scene from the film with music and then without music. I couldn't believe the difference.

The first time I watched the film, I didn't even notice that music was playing. I was just on the edge of my seat waiting and hoping that things would turn out the way I wanted them to. When I watched it without music, the scene was flat. There wasn't the same level of anticipation. Without music it felt factual, not emotional.

Whether it's a hymn at church, a college fight song, a song on the radio, or the carefully scored soundtrack to a movie, music reaches out and offers us connection—something we really can't live without.

DANCING

I measure the spiritual health of our family by how much dancing is happening in our kitchen. Some days it's Lizzo and Lyle Lovett; some days it's an entire routine to Vanilla Ice. And we don't have a big kitchen so when the four of us are in there, sock-footed and sliding around, it looks more like a mosh pit than a sock hop. It's messy, but it's always fun.

It didn't take me long to learn that dance is a tough issue for many people. Laughing hysterically can make us feel a little out of control, and singing out loud can make some of us feel self-conscious. But for many of us, there is no form of self-expression that makes us feel more vulnerable than dancing. It's literally full-body vulnerability. The only other full-body vulnerability that I can think of is being naked, and I don't have to tell you how vulnerable that makes most of us feel.

For many people, risking that kind of public vulnerability is too difficult, so they dance at home or only in front of people they care about. For others, the vulnerability is so crushing that they don't dance at all. One woman told me, "Sometimes if I'm watching TV and people are dancing or there's a good song playing, I tap my feet without even noticing it. When I finally catch myself, I feel embarrassed. I have no rhythm."

There's no question that some people are more musically inclined or coordinated than others, but I'm starting to believe that dance is in our DNA. Not super-hip and cool dancing, or line dancing, or *Dancing with the Stars* dancing—but a strong pull toward rhythm and movement. You can see this desire to move in children. *Until* we teach our children that they need to be concerned with how they look and with what other people think, they dance. They even dance naked. Not always gracefully or with the beat, but always with joy and pleasure.

Writer Mary Jo Putney says, "What one loves in childhood stays in the heart forever." If this is true, and I believe it is, then dance stays in our heart, even when our head becomes overly concerned with what people might think.

BEING COOL AND "ALWAYS IN CONTROL"

The only true currency in this bankrupt world
is what you share with someone else when
you're uncool.

—A QUOTE FROM THE FILM
Almost Famous, 2000

A good belly laugh, singing at the top of your lungs, and dancing like no one is looking are unquestionably good for the
soul. But as I mentioned, they are also exercises in vulnerability. There are many shame triggers around the vulnerability
of laughing, song, and dance. The list includes the fear of
being perceived as awkward, goofy, silly, spastic, uncool, out
of control, immature, stupid, and foolish. For most of us, this
is a pretty scary list. The gremlins are constantly there to
make sure that self-expression takes a backseat to self-
protection and self-consciousness.

- "What will people think?"
- "Everyone is watching—calm down!"
- "You look ridiculous! Get a hold of yourself."

Women spoke about the dangers of being perceived as
"getting too loud" or "out of hand." I can't tell you how many
women told me about the painful experience of throwing caution to the wind, only to be patronizingly told, "Whoa . . .
settle down."

Men were quick to point out the dangers of being perceived as "out of control." One man told me, "Women say we
should let loose and have fun. How attractive will they think
we are if we get out on the dance floor and look like assholes
in front of other guys—or worse—your girlfriend's friends?
It's easier to just hang back and act like you're not interested
in dancing. Even if you really want to."

There are many ways in which we hustle for worthiness
around these issues, but the two that keep us the most quiet
and still are hustling to be perceived as "cool" and "in con-

trol." Wanting to be perceived as cool is our effort to minimize vulnerability in order to reduce the risk of being ridiculed or made fun of.

We hustle for our worthiness by slipping on the emotional and behavioral straitjacket of cool and posturing as the tragically hip and the terminally "better than." Being "in control" isn't always about the desire to manipulate situations, but often it's about the need to manage perception. We want to be able to control what other people think about us so that we can feel good enough.

I grew up in a family where being cool and fitting in were highly valued. As an adult, I have to constantly work at allowing myself to be vulnerable and authentic around some of these issues. I could laugh and sing and dance as an adult, as long as I stayed clear of silly, goofy, and awkward. For years, these were major shame triggers for me.

During my 2007 ~~Breakdown~~ Spiritual Awakening, I learned how much I've missed while pretending to be cool. I realized that one of the reasons I'm afraid to try new things (like yoga or the hip-hop exercise class at my gym) is my fear of being perceived as goofy and awkward.

I've spent a lot of time and energy working on this. It's a slow process. I'm still only super-silly and goofy around people I trust, but I think that's okay. I'm also working hard not to pass this down to my kids. It's easy to do when we're not mindful of the gremlins and shame triggers. Here's proof:

Many years ago, when Ellen was still in grade school, I had to run to Nordstrom to pick up some makeup. I was in one of those "nothing fits and I feel like Jabba the Hutt" moods, so I put on my baggiest sweats, pulled my dirty hair back with a headband, and told Ellen, "We're just running in and running out."

On the way to the mall, Ellen reminded me that the shoes her grandmother had bought her were in the back of the car and asked if we could exchange them for a bigger size while we were at the store. After I bought my makeup, we went upstairs to the kids' shoe department. As soon as we cleared the top of the escalator, I saw a trio of gorgeous women standing in the shoe department. They were tossing their long (clean) hair over their narrow, square shoulders as they perched on their high-heeled, pointed-toe boots and watched their equally beautiful daughters try on sneakers.

As I tried to avoid crumbling and comparing by focusing on the display shoes, I saw a strange blur of jerky movement out of the corner of my eye. It was Ellen. A pop song was playing in the neighboring children's department, and Ellen, my totally confident eight-year-old, was dancing. Or, to be more specific, she was doing the robot.

At the very moment that Ellen looked up and saw me watching her, I saw the magnificent moms and their matching daughters staring right at Ellen. The mothers looked embarrassed for her, and the daughters, who were a couple of years older than Ellen, were visibly on the edge of doing or saying something mean-spirited. Ellen froze. Still bent over with her arms in rigid formation, she looked up at me with eyes that said, "What do I do, Mom?"

My default response in this scenario is to shoot a diminishing look at Ellen that says, "Geez, man. Don't be so uncool!" Basically, my immediate reaction would be to save myself by betraying Ellen. Thank God I didn't. Some combination of being immersed in this work, having a mother instinct that was louder than my fear, and pure grace told me, "Choose Ellen! Be on her side!"

I glanced up at the other mothers and then looked at Ellen. I reached down into my courage, as far as I go, smiled, and said, "You need to add the scarecrow to your moves." I let my wrist and hand dangle from my extended arm and pretended to bat my forearm around. Ellen smiled. We stood in the middle of the shoe department and practiced our moves until the song was over. I'm not sure how the onlookers responded to our shoe department Soul Train. I didn't take my eyes off Ellen.

Betrayal is an important word with this guidepost. When we value being cool and in control over granting ourselves the freedom to unleash the passionate, goofy, heartfelt, and soulful expressions of who we are, we betray ourselves. When we consistently betray ourselves, we can expect to do the same to the people we love.

When we don't give ourselves permission to be free, we rarely tolerate that freedom in others. We put them down, make fun of them, ridicule their behaviors, and sometimes shame them. We can do this intentionally or unconsciously. Either way the message is, "Geez, man. Don't be so uncool."

The Hopi Indians have a saying, "To watch us dance is to hear our hearts speak." I know how much courage it takes to let people hear our hearts speak, but life is way too precious to spend it pretending like we're super-cool and totally in control when we could be laughing, singing, and dancing.

DIG DEEP

Get Deliberate: If we believe that laughter, song, and dance are essential to our soul-care, how do we make sure that we hold space for them in our lives? One thing that we've started doing is turning on music in the kitchen while we do a family cleanup after supper. We dance and sing, which in turn, always leads to a good laugh.

Get Inspired: I love making "themed playlists"—groups of songs that I want to listen to when I'm feeling a certain way. I have everything from a playlist called "God on the iPod" to a "Run like you mean it" list. My favorite is my "Authentic Me" list—the songs that make me feel most like myself.

Get Going: Dare to be goofy. Dance every day for five minutes. Make a CD of songs to sing along with in the car. Watch that fun TikTok video that makes you laugh every time!

Final Thoughts

I think most of us have developed fairly sensitive bullshit meters when it comes to reading "self-help" books. I think this is a good thing. There are too many books that make promises they can't keep or make change sound so much easier than it is. The truth is that meaningful change is a process. It can be uncomfortable and is often risky, especially when we're talking about embracing our imperfections, cultivating authenticity, and looking the world in the eye and saying, "I am enough."

However afraid we are of change, the question that we must ultimately answer is this: *What's the greater risk? Letting go of what people think or letting go of how I feel, what I believe, and who I am?*

Wholehearted living is about engaging in our lives from a place of worthiness. It's about cultivating the courage, compassion, and connection to wake up in the morning and think, *No matter what gets done and how much is left undone, I am enough.* It's going to bed at night thinking, *Yes, I am imperfect and vulnerable and sometimes afraid, but that doesn't change the truth that I am also brave and worthy of love and belonging.*

It makes sense to me that the gifts of imperfection are courage, compassion, and connection, because when I think back to my life before this work, I remember often feeling fearful, judgmental, and alone—the opposite of the gifts. I wondered, *What if I can't keep all of these balls in the air? Why isn't everyone else working harder and living up to my expectations? What will people think if I fail or give up? When can I stop proving myself to everyone?*

For me, the risk of losing myself felt far more dangerous than the risk of letting people see the real me. With the 10th Anniversary edition of this book, it's been fourteen years since that day in 2006 when my own research turned my life upside down. It's been the best fourteen years of my life, and I wouldn't change a thing. The ~~Breakdown~~ Spiritual Awakening was tough, but I'm hardheaded. I guess the universe needed a way to get my attention.

Despite where this book will be shelved in your local bookstore, I'm not at all sure that this work is about self-help. I think of it as an invitation to join a wholehearted revolution. A small, quiet, grassroots movement that starts with each of us saying, "My story matters because I matter." A movement where we can take to the streets with our messy, imperfect, wild, stretch-marked, wonderful, heartbreaking, grace-filled, and joyful lives. A movement fueled by the freedom that comes when we stop pretending that everything is okay when it isn't. A call that rises up from our bellies when we find the courage to celebrate those intensely joyful moments even though we've convinced ourselves that savoring happiness is inviting disaster.

Revolution might sound a little dramatic, but in this world, choosing authenticity and worthiness is an absolute act of resistance. Choosing to live and love with our whole hearts is an act of defiance. You're going to confuse, piss off, and terrify lots of people—including yourself. One minute you'll pray that the transformation stops, and the next minute you'll pray that it never ends. You'll also wonder how you can feel so brave and so afraid at the same time. At least that's how I feel most of the time . . . brave, afraid, and very, very alive.

About the Research Process

For Thrill-Seekers and Methodology Junkies

Many years ago, a young woman came up to me after a speaking event and said, "I hope you won't think this is weird or rude or something, but you don't look like a researcher." She didn't say anything else; she just stood there waiting and looking confused.

I smiled and asked, "What do you mean?"

She replied, "You seem so normal."

I chuckled. "Well, looks can be deceiving. I'm so *not* normal."

We ended up having a great conversation. She was a single mother getting her undergraduate degree in psychology and loved her research classes, but her faculty advisor wasn't encouraging her to pursue the research track. We talked about work and motherhood and what researchers are supposed to look like. It seemed that I was missing the mice, the long white lab coat, and the Y chromosome. She told me, "I pictured older white guys working in labs and studying mice, not a soccer mom studying feelings."

The journey that led me to become a researcher was anything but a straight and narrow path, which, ironically, is probably why and how I ended up studying human behavior and emotion for a living. I was a college drop-in and drop-out for a number of years. During my "off semesters," I waited tables and tended bar, hitchhiked through Europe, played a lot of tennis . . . you get the point.

I found the social work profession in my late twenties and knew it was home. I did a two-year stint in junior colleges to raise my GPA enough to get into a big university with a social work program. It was in those junior college classes that I fell in love with the idea of teaching and writing.

After years of dropping out, I graduated with honors from the University of Texas–Austin with my bachelor's degree in social work when I was twenty-nine and immediately applied for graduate school at the University of Houston. I got accepted, worked hard and finished my master's, and was accepted into the doctoral program.

During my doctoral studies, I discovered qualitative research. Unlike quantitative research, which is about tests and statistics that give you what you need to predict and control phenomena, qualitative research is about finding patterns and themes that help you better understand the phenomenon you're studying. They're equally important approaches but very different.

I use a specific qualitative methodology called Grounded Theory.[1] I was fortunate enough to be trained by Barney Glaser, one of the two men who developed the methodology in the 1960s. Dr. Glaser commuted from California to serve as the methodologist on my dissertation committee.

The basic premise of Grounded Theory research is to start with as few preconceived ideas and assumptions as possible so that you can build a theory based on the data that emerges from the process. For example, when I first started with what I would later refer to as Wholehearted Research, I had two questions: What is the anatomy of human connection, and how does it work? After studying the best and worst of humanity, I had learned that nothing is as important as human connection and I wanted to know more about the ins and outs of how we develop meaningful connections.

In the process of collecting data to answer the questions, I ran into shame—this thing that corroded connection. I decided to take a quick detour to understand shame so that I could better understand connection. At that point, my questions became, "What is shame, and how does it affect our lives?"

My quick detour turned into eight years (there was lots to learn). I posed new questions based on what I had learned: The research participants who had embraced their vulnerabilities and imperfections and developed a powerful level of resilience to shame seemed to value a certain way of living. What did they value, and how did they cultivate what they needed? These questions became the basis for determining what it takes for most people to live with their whole hearts.

My data doesn't come from questionnaires or surveys; I interview people and collect stories using field notes. I'm basically a story catcher. When the first edition of this book was published, I had collected more than ten thousand stories. I'd done formal research interviews with close to one thousand participants individually and in focus groups. People shared their stories with me through letters, email, my blog, and the courses I've taught. Some have even sent me their art and copies of their journals. I've also presented to tens of thousands of mental health professionals who have shared their case studies with me.

When I'm finished interviewing, I analyze the stories for themes and patterns so I can generate theories from the data. When I code data (analyze the stories), I go into deep researcher mode where my only focus is on accurately capturing what I heard in the stories. I don't think about how I would say something, only how they said it. I don't think about what an experience would mean to me, only what it meant to the person who told me about it.

Rather than approaching a problem and saying, "I need to collect evidence of what I know to be true," the Grounded Theory approach forces me to let go of my interests and investments so I can focus on the concerns, interests, and ideas of the people I interview.

The data-coding process is laborious and difficult. My husband, Steve, likes to leave town with the kids when I go into my comparing, coding, memoing phase. He says it's kind of scary because I walk around the house dazed and mumbling with a stack of yellow legal pads in my hands. It's a very attractive process.

What I love/hate the most about Grounded Theory is that it's never really done. The theory that you generate from your data is only as "good" as its ability to explain new data. That means every time you collect a new story or a new piece of information, you have to hold it up against the theory you've developed. Does it work? Does it ring true? Does your existing theory work this new data in a meaningful way?

If you follow my work, you can probably attest to the evolving nature of my theory-building. If you want to honor the stories that people have shared with you, you have to stay rigorous in your attempts to accurately capture their meaning. It's a challenge, but I honestly love what I do.

If you're really interested in Grounded Theory or if you want more information on methodology, visit my Web site for links to the academic articles on Shame Resilience Theory (brenebrown.com).

Acknowledgments

To the BBEARG Team: Suzanne Barrall, Cookie Boeker, Gracie Cuevas, Ronda Dearing, Lauren Emmerson, Margarita Flores, Lauren Smith Ford, Barrett Guillen, Kat Hubbs, Charles Kiley, Tré LeDay, Bryan Longoria, Murdoch Mackinnon, Laura Mayes, Tati Reznick, Gabi Rodriquez, Deanne Rogers, Ashley Brown Ruiz, Teresa Sample, Kathryn Schultz, Anne Stoeber, and Genia Williams: Keep being brave, serving the work, and taking good care. You make me a braver person and I learn from all of you every single day. Thank you. #theworkwedo

To my editor, Ben Greenberg: Thank you for chasing me down, making me laugh, and missing cigarettes with me.

To the Random House team of Gina Centrello, Andy Ward, Molly Turpin, Theresa Zoro, Maria Braeckel, Melissa Sanford, Erin Richards, Leigh Marchant, Jessica Bonet, Benjamin Dreyer, Loren Noveck, Barbara M. Bachman, Joe Perez, Sandra Sjursen, Emily DeHuff, Lisa Feuer, and Karen Dziekonski.

To Jennifer Rudolph Walsh, Tracy Fisher, Suzanne Gluck, and the WME team: Thank you for the grit, grind, and grace.

To Brandi Bernoskie and the team at Alchemy + Aim: Thank you for bringing it all to life!

To the Global Prairie team of Wendy Hauser, Mike Hauser, and Kristin Enyart: On to the next chapter (and cover!)!

Love and thanks to Deanne Rogers; Chuck Brown; Jacobina Alley; Corky and Jack Crisci; Ashley and Amaya Ruiz; Barrett, Frankie, and Gabi Guillen; Jason and Layla Brown; Jen, David, Larkin, and Pierce Alley; Shif Berhanu; Negash Berhanu; Margarita Flores: I love y'all.

To Polly Koch: I miss you.

To Steve, Ellen, Charlie, and Lucy: My heart and home.

Notes

PREFACE

1. Brené Brown, *Connections: A 12-Session Psychoeducational Shame-Resilience Curriculum* (Center City, MN: Hazelden, 2009); Brené Brown, *I Thought It Was Just Me (but it isn't): Telling the Truth About Perfectionism, Inadequacy, and Power* (New York: Penguin / Gotham Books, 2007); Brené Brown, "Shame Resilience Theory," in *Contemporary Human Behavior Theory: A Critical Perspective for Social Work*, rev. ed., ed. Susan P. Robbins, Pranab Chatterjee, and Edward R. Canda (Boston: Allyn and Bacon, 2007); Brené Brown, "Shame Resilience Theory: A Grounded Theory Study on Women and Shame," *Families in Society* 87, no. 1 (2006): 43–52.

INTRODUCTION:
WHOLEHEARTED LIVING

1. Stuart Brown with Christopher Vaughan, *Play: How It Shapes the Brain, Opens the Imagination, and Invigorates the Soul* (New York: Penguin Group, 2009).

COURAGE, COMPASSION, AND CONNECTION:
THE GIFTS OF IMPERFECTION

1. I'm not sure where the term *ordinary courage* first appeared, but I discovered it in an article on women and girls by researcher Annie Rogers.
2. Pema Chödrön, *The Places That Scare You: A Guide to Fearlessness in Difficult Times* (Boston: Shambhala Publications, 2001).
3. Ibid.
4. Daniel Goleman, *Social Intelligence: The New Science of*

Human Relationships (New York: Random House / Bantam Dell, 2006).

EXPLORING THE POWER OF LOVE, BELONGING,
AND BEING ENOUGH

1. bell hooks, *All About Love: New Visions* (New York: Harper-Collins Publishers, Harper Paperbacks, 2001).
2. Blog comment used with permission from Justin Valentin.
3. Blog comment used with permission from Renae Cobb.

THE THINGS THAT GET IN THE WAY

1. Brené Brown, *I Thought It Was Just Me (but it isn't): Telling the Truth About Perfectionism, Inadequacy, and Power* (New York: Penguin / Gotham Books, 2007).
2. The most comprehensive review of the current research literature on shame and guilt can be found in *Shame and Guilt* by June Price Tangney and Ronda L. Dearing (New York: Guilford Press, 2002).
3. Linda M. Hartling, Wendy Rosen, Maureen Walker, and Judith V. Jordan, *Shame and Humiliation: From Isolation to Relational Transformation,* Work in Progress No. 88 (Wellesley, MA: The Stone Center, Wellesley College, 2000).

GUIDEPOST #1, CULTIVATING AUTHENTICITY:
LETTING GO OF WHAT PEOPLE THINK

1. James R. Mahalik, Elisabeth B. Morray, Aimée Coonerty-Femiano, Larry H. Ludlow, Suzanne M. Slattery, and Andrew Smiler, "Development of the Conformity to Feminine Norms Inventory," *Sex Roles* 52, no. 7–8 (2005): 417–35.
2. James R. Mahalik, W. Tracy Talmadge, Benjamin D. Locke, and Ryan P. J. Scott, "Using the Conformity to Masculine Norms Inventory to Work with Men in a Clinical Setting," *Journal of Clinical Psychology* 61, no. 6 (2005): 661–74; James R. Mahalik, Benjamin D. Locke, Larry H. Ludlow, Matthew A. Diemer, Ryan P. J. Scott, Michael Gottfried, and Gary Freitas, "Development of the Conformity to Masculine Norms Inventory," *Psychology of Men and Masculinity* 4, no. 1 (2003): 3–25.
3. Katherine Center blog, essay for *Defining a Movement* video, posted January 28, 2010, www.katherinecenter.com/defining-a-movement/.

GUIDEPOST #2, CULTIVATING SELF-COMPASSION:
LETTING GO OF PERFECTIONISM

1. Anna Quindlen, "Anna Quindlen's Commencement Speech," www.mtholyoke.edu/offices/comm/oped/Quindlen.shtml; Anna Quindlen, *Being Perfect* (New York: Random House, 2005).
2. Joe Scott, "The Effect of Perfectionism and Unconditional Self-Acceptance on Depression," *Journal of Rational-Emotive and Cognitive-Behavior Therapy* 25, no. 1 (2007): 35–64; Anna M. Bardone-Cone, Katrina Sturm, Melissa A. Lawson, D. Paul Robinson, and Roma Smith, "Perfectionism across Stages of Recovery from Eating Disorders," *International Journal of Eating Disorders* 43, no. 2 (2010): 139–48; Hyunjoo Park, P. Paul Heppner, and Dong-gwi Lee, "Maladaptive Coping and Self-Esteem as Mediators between Perfectionism and Psychological Distress," *Personality and Individual Differences* 48, no. 4 (March 2010): 469–74.
3. Christopher K. Germer, *The Mindful Path to Self-Compassion: Freeing Yourself from Destructive Thoughts and Emotions* (New York: Guilford Press, 2009).
4. Kristin D. Neff, "Self-Compassion: An Alternative Conceptualization of a Healthy Attitude Toward Oneself," *Self and Identity* 2 (2003): 85–101.
5. Kristin D. Neff, "The Development and Validation of a Scale to Measure Self-Compassion," *Self and Identity* 2 (2003): 223–50.
6. Leonard Cohen, "Anthem," *The Future,* 1992, Columbia Records.

GUIDEPOST #3, CULTIVATING
A RESILIENT SPIRIT: LETTING GO OF NUMBING
AND POWERLESSNESS

1. Used with permission from Terri St. Cloud.
2. Suniya S. Luthar, Dante Cicchetti, and Bronwyn Becker, "The Construct of Resilience: A Critical Evaluation and Guidelines for Future Work," *Child Development* 71, no. 3 (2000): 543–62; Suniya S. Luthar and Dante Cicchetti, "The Construct of Resilience: Implications for Interventions and Social Policies," *Development and Psychopathology* 12 (2000): 857–85; Christine E. Agaibi and John P. Wilson, "Trauma, PTSD, and Resilience: A Review of the Literature," *Trauma, Violence, and Abuse* 6, no. 3 (2005): 195–216; Anthony D. Ong, C. S. Bergeman, Toni L. Bisconti, and Kimberly A. Wallace, "Psychological Resilience, Positive Emotions, and Successful Adaptation

to Stress in Later Life," *Journal of Personality and Social Psychology* 91, no. 4 (2006): 730–49.

3.   C. R. Snyder, *Psychology of Hope: You Can Get There from Here,* paperback ed. (New York: Free Press, 2003); C. R. Snyder, "Hope Theory: Rainbows in the Mind," *Psychological Inquiry* 13, no. 4 (2002): 249–75.

4.   C. R. Snyder, Kenneth A. Lehman, Ben Kluck, and Yngve Monsson, "Hope for Rehabilitation and Vice Versa," *Rehabilitation Psychology* 51, no. 2 (2006): 89–112; C. R. Snyder, "Hope Theory: Rainbows in the Mind," *Psychological Inquiry* 13, no. 4 (2002): 249–75.

5.   Gerard J. Connors, Stephen A. Maisto, and William H. Zywiak, "Male and Female Alcoholics' Attributions Regarding the Onset and Termination of Relapses and the Maintenance of Abstinence," *Journal of Substance Abuse* 10, no. 1 (1998): 27–42; G. Alan Marlatt and Dennis M. Donovan, *Relapse Prevention: Maintenance Strategies in the Treatment of Addictive Behaviors,* 2nd ed. (New York: Guilford Press, 2007); Norman S. Miller and Mark S. Gold, "Dissociation of 'Conscious Desire' (Craving) from and Relapse in Alcohol and Cocaine Dependence," *Annals of Clinical Psychology* 6, no. 2 (1994): 99–106.

GUIDEPOST #4, CULTIVATING GRATITUDE AND JOY: LETTING GO OF SCARCITY AND FEAR OF THE DARK

1.   Anne Robertson, "Joy or Happiness?" St. John's United Methodist Church, stjohnsdover.org/99adv3.html. Used with permission from Anne Robertson.

2.   Lynne Twist, *The Soul of Money: Transforming Your Relationship with Money and Life* (New York: W. W. Norton and Company, 2003), 44.

3.   Ibid., 75.

4.   Brené Brown, *I Thought It Was Just Me (but it isn't): Telling the Truth About Perfectionism, Inadequacy, and Power* (New York: Penguin / Gotham Books, 2007), 204–205.

GUIDEPOST #5, CULTIVATING INTUITION AND TRUSTING FAITH: LETTING GO OF THE NEED FOR CERTAINTY

1.   "Intuition," www.Dictionary.com (accessed February 17, 2010).

2.   David G. Myers, *Intuition: Its Powers and Perils* (New Haven, CT: Yale University Press, 2002); Gerd Gigerenzer, *Gut Feelings: The Intelligence of the Unconscious* (London: Penguin Books, 2008).

3.   Richard Rohr, "Utterly Humbled by Mystery," published December 18, 2006, National Public Radio "This I Believe" series, www .npr.org/templates/story/story.php?storyId=6631954 (accessed February 15, 2010).

4.   Anne Lamott, *Plan B: Further Thoughts on Faith*, paperback ed. (New York: Penguin Group, Riverhead Books, 2006), 256–57.

5.   Anne Lamott, *Bird by Bird: Some Instructions on Writing and Life* (New York: Random House, Anchor Books, 1995); Anne Lamott, *Grace (Eventually): Thoughts on Faith*, paperback ed. (New York: Penguin Group, Riverhead Books, 2008).

6.   Sue Monk Kidd, *When the Heart Waits: Spiritual Direction for Life's Sacred Questions* (New York: HarperCollins, HarperOne, 2006).

7.   Pema Chödrön, *Comfortable with Uncertainty: 108 Teachings on Cultivating Fearlessness and Compassion*, mass market ed. (Boston, MA: Shambhala Publications, 2008).

8.   Paulo Coelho, *The Alchemist* (New York: HarperCollins, 2006).

GUIDEPOST #7, CULTIVATING PLAY AND REST:
LETTING GO OF EXHAUSTION AS A STATUS SYMBOL
AND PRODUCTIVITY AS SELF-WORTH

1.   Stuart Brown with Christopher Vaughan, *Play: How It Shapes the Brain, Opens the Imagination, and Invigorates the Soul* (New York: Penguin Group, 2009).

2.   Ibid.

3.   "Sleep and Sleep Disorders: A Public Health Challenge," www. cdc.gov/sleep/; L. R. McKnight-Eily and others, "Perceived Insufficient Rest or Sleep—Four States, 2006," *MMWR (Morbidity and Mortality Weekly Report)* 57, no. 8 (February 29, 2008): 200–203, www.cdc.gov/mmwr/preview/mmwrhtml/mm5708a2.htm (accessed January 2, 2010), analyzed data from CDC's Behavioral Risk Factor Surveillance System (BRFSS).

4.   Daniel H. Pink, *A Whole New Mind: Why Right-Brainers Will Rule the Future*, paperback ed. (New York: Penguin Group, Riverhead Books, 2006).

GUIDEPOST #8, CULTIVATING CALM AND STILLNESS:
LETTING GO OF ANXIETY AS A LIFESTYLE

1.   Maude Bryt, *Baby Love: A Tradition of Calm Parenting* (New York: Dell, 1998).

2.   Harriet Lerner, *The Dance of Connection: How to Talk to*

Someone When You're Mad, Hurt, Scared, Frustrated, Insulted, Betrayed, or Desperate (New York: HarperCollins, 2002).
   3.   Ibid.

GUIDEPOST #9, CULTIVATING MEANINGFUL WORK:
LETTING GO OF SELF-DOUBT AND "SUPPOSED TO"

   1.   Marci Alboher, *One Person/Multiple Careers: A New Model for Work/Life Success* (New York: Business Plus, 2007).
   2.   Malcolm Gladwell, *Outliers: The Story of Success* (New York: Hachette Book Group, Little, Brown and Company, 2008).
   3.   Paulo Coelho, *The Alchemist* (New York: HarperCollins, 2006).

GUIDEPOST #10, CULTIVATING LAUGHTER,
SONG, AND DANCE: LETTING GO OF BEING COOL
AND "ALWAYS IN CONTROL"

   1.   Barbara Ehrenreich, *Dancing in the Streets: A History of Collective Joy* (New York: Metropolitan Books, 2006).

ABOUT THE RESEARCH PROCESS:
A CHAPTER FOR THRILL-SEEKERS AND
METHODOLOGY JUNKIES

   1.   Barney G. Glaser and Anselm L. Strauss, *The Discovery of Grounded Theory: Strategies for Qualitative Research* (Hawthorne, NY: Aldine Transaction, 1967); Barney G. Glaser, *Theoretical Sensitivity: Advances in the Methodology of Grounded Theory* (Mill Valley, CA: Sociology Press, 1978); Barney G. Glaser, *Basics of Grounded Theory Analysis: Emergence vs. Forcing* (Mill Valley, CA: Sociology Press, 1992); Barney G. Glaser, *Doing Grounded Theory: Issues and Discussions* (Mill Valley, CA: Sociology Press, 1998); Barney G. Glaser, *The Grounded Theory Perspective: Conceptualization Contrasted with Description* (Mill Valley, CA: Sociology Press, 2001); Barney G. Glaser, *The Grounded Theory Perspective II: Description's Remodeling of Grounded Theory* (Mill Valley, CA: Sociology Press, 2003); Barney G. Glaser, *The Grounded Theory Perspective III: Theoretical Coding* (Mill Valley, CA: Sociology Press, 2005).

DR. BRENÉ BROWN is a research professor at the University of Houston, where she holds the Huffington Foundation–Brené Brown Endowed Chair at the Graduate College of Social Work. Brené is also a visiting professor in management at The University of Texas at Austin's Mc-Combs School of Business.

She has spent the past two decades studying courage, vulnerability, shame, and empathy and is the author of five #1 *New York Times* best-sellers: *The Gifts of Imperfection, Daring Greatly, Rising Strong, Braving the Wilderness,* and her latest book, *Dare to Lead,* which is the culmination of a seven-year study on courage and leadership.

Brené hosts the *Unlocking Us* podcast, and her TEDx talk—"The Power of Vulnerability"—is one of the top five most-viewed TED talks in the world with more than 50 million views. She is also the first re-searcher to have a filmed lecture on Netflix. *The Call to Courage* de-buted on the streaming service on April 19, 2019.

Brené lives in Houston, Texas, with her husband, Steve. They have two children, Ellen and Charlie, and a weird bichon named Lucy.

brenebrown.com

Facebook.com/brenebrown

Twitter: @BreneBrown

Instagram: @BreneBrown

Welcome to Your

INTEGRATION

INDEX

Integrating

First, if you haven't completed the free Wholehearted Inventory, this is a great time to do it. You can find it at brene brown.com/wholeheartedinventory.

Second, please join us for a free online workshop on *The Gifts of Imperfection* at brenebrown.com/thegifts. You can dig in from anywhere!

Now let's set up your integration index. This is a personal process, so rather than assigning categories for you to index, I've provided a list of suggestions and blank pages for you to make this process your own. Always feel free to add or change as you move through the book.

When you come across something that's important to you, highlight and tag it. Then write the page number under the related index category. When you're done, you haven't just read the book, you've inhabited it. There's no secret message in your completed index—the process of doing this is the integration work.

In other words, simply slowing down; rereading something that resonates with you, frustrates you, or maybe even confuses you; highlighting and tagging it; then figuring out why it's important and where you want to file that in your mind, in your life, and in your index—this process is the engine of integration.

Here are some suggestions. They're in alphabetical order because that's how I usually do my indexes, so I can find the subject headings faster.

THESE ARE STANDARDS THAT I USE IN ALMOST ALL MY BOOKS:

- Beautiful words:
- Definitions (there are a lot of definitions in this book):
- I don't get it:
- I want to work on this:
- Quotes:
- Read more:
- SO HARD:
- Takeaways:
- Talk about with _____:
- Dig into research (always on my nerd alert):

The book-specific topics will always vary according to the themes of each particular book. Here are some example topics for *The Gifts*.

- At work:
- Belonging:
- Love:
- Parenting:
- Perfectionism:
- Shame:
- Vulnerability:

LET'S GET STARTED!

INTEGRATION

Idea:

PAGE NUMBERS:

NOTES:

INTEGRATION

Idea:

PAGE NUMBERS:

NOTES:

INTEGRATION

Idea:

PAGE NUMBERS:

NOTES:

INTEGRATION

Idea:

PAGE NUMBERS:

NOTES:

INTEGRATION

Idea:

PAGE NUMBERS:

NOTES:

INTEGRATION

Idea:

PAGE NUMBERS:

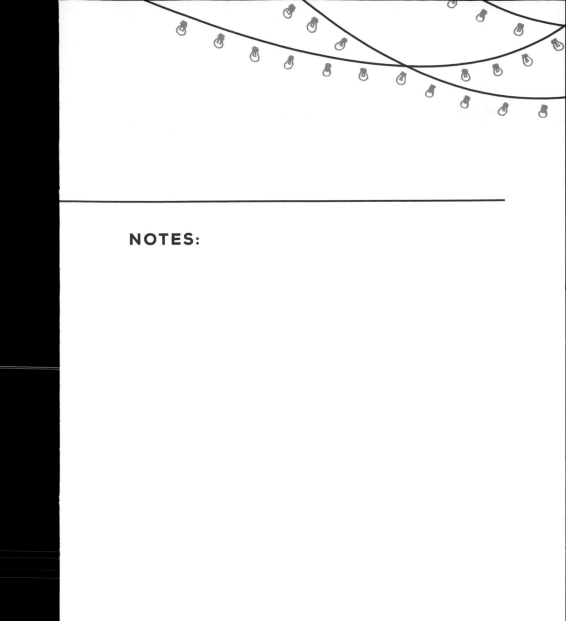

NOTES:

INTEGRATION

Idea:

PAGE NUMBERS:

NOTES:

INTEGRATION

Idea:

PAGE NUMBERS:

NOTES:

INTEGRATION

Idea:

PAGE NUMBERS:

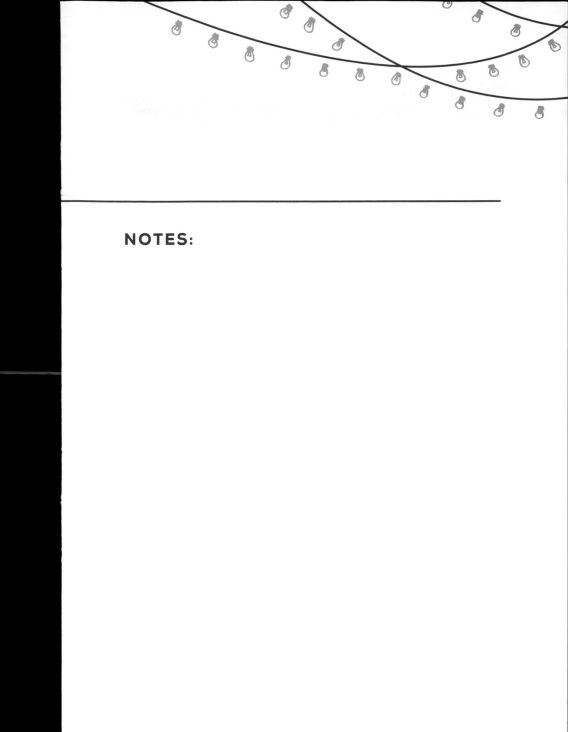

NOTES:

INTEGRATION

Idea:

PAGE NUMBERS:

NOTES:

NOTES:

NOTES:

NOTES:

NOTES: